Cambridge Opera Handbooks

W. A. Mozart
Idomeneo

Published titles

W. A. Mozart
Idomeneo

JULIAN RUSHTON

CAMBRIDGE
UNIVERSITY PRESS

Published by the Press Syndicate of the University of Cambridge
The Pitt Building, Trumpington Street, Cambridge CB2 IRP
40 West 20th Street, New York, NY 10011–4211, USA
10 Stamford Road, Oakleigh, Melbourne 3166, Australia

© Cambridge University Press 1993

First published 1993

Printed in Great Britain at the University Press, Cambridge

A catalogue record for this book is available from the British Library

Library of Congress cataloguing in publication data

Rushton, Julian
W. A. Mozart, Idomeneo/Julian Rushton.
p.   cm. – (Cambridge opera handbooks)
Includes bibliographical references and index.
ISBN 0 521 43144 1 (hardback). – ISBN 0 521 43741 5 (pbk.)
1. Mozart, Wolfgang Amadeus, 1756–1791. Idomeneo. I. title.
II. Title: Idomeneo. III. Series.
ML410.M9R89   1983
782. 1 – dc20   92–25833   CIP   MN

ISBN 0 521 43144 1 hardback
ISBN 0 521 43741 5 paperback

SN

For Virginia

Contents

Illustrations

viii

General preface

This is a series of studies of individual operas, written for the serious opera-goer or record-collector as well as the student or scholar. Each volume has three main concerns. The first is historical: to describe the genesis of the work, its sources or its relation to literary proto-types, the collaboration between librettist and composer, and the first performance and subsequent stage history. The history is itself a record of changing attitudes towards the work, and an index of general changes of taste. The second is analytical and it is grounded in a very full synopsis which considers the opera as a structure of musical and dramatic effects. In most volumes there is also a musical analysis of a section of the score, showing how the music serves or makes the drama. The analysis, like the history, naturally raises questions of interpretation, and the third concern of each volume is to show how critical writing about an opera, like production and performance, can direct or distort appreciation of its structural elements. Some conflict or interpretation is an inevitable part of this account; editors of the handbooks reflect this – by citing classic statements, by commissioning new essays, by taking up their own critical position. A final section gives a select bibliography and guides to other sources.

Acknowledgements

I am grateful to my colleagues who have written parts of this volume, notably Stanley Sadie, who contributed many helpful observations arising out of work on *The New Grove Dictionary of Opera*. All the contributors suffered my editorial interventions graciously, and provided helpful comments on my own work. Chris Walton helped with obtaining the libretto and illustrations. I also owe much to those whose work does not appear, in particular the leading English-speaking *Idomeneo* scholar, Daniel Heartz, for friendly encouragement at the inception of the project; a book on *Idomeneo* with no contribution from him may seem incomplete, but the reader is invited to follow up our many references to his work. Among others invited but unable to contribute I wish particularly to thank Alan Tyson for comments on the autograph; Esther Cavett-Dunsby and David Cairns for many illuminating comments. For supplying information or communicating unpublished material, we all thank Cliff Eisen, Daniel Heartz, Robert Münster and Lois Rosow. At Cambridge University Press, I would like to thank Michael Black, Penny Souster, and Victoria Cooper for valued comments and general assistance, as well as great patience. I am particularly grateful to Alison Stonehouse for perusing the script, for whose remaining shortcomings I alone am responsible.

Introduction

When he composed *Idomeneo* Mozart was not quite twenty-five, yet it is his tenth completed opera. It followed two serious operas, *Mitridate, re di Ponto* and *Lucio Silla*, written for Milan; the courtly allegories *Ascanio in Alba* and *Il sogno di Scipione*, for Milan and Salzburg; and *Il rè pastore*, for Salzburg in 1775. In these works there is scarcely a moment of levity: they deal in heroism, love, loyalty, magnanimity, and affairs of state. Despite two comedies written when he was twelve, and the Munich *opera buffa La finta giardiniera*, comedy played a comparatively small role in Mozart's early operatic output.

Idomeneo stands at a watershed in Mozart's career, but it also stands alone. It is the first of his mature operas rather than the last of his youth: thereafter he wrote only one *opera seria*, *La clemenza di Tito*. *Idomeneo* falls between two oriental adventure operas in German, the grave and unfinished *Zaide* (*c.* 1779) and *Die Entführung aus dem Serail*, performed in Vienna in 1782. It bears surprisingly little relationship in technique to the earlier Italian operas. *Mitridate*, *Lucio Silla*, and *Il re pastore* conform to the traditional type of *opera seria* in which there is no supernatural intervention; the plots are fiction, the characters historical, and the score consists almost entirely of recitative and arias. *Idomeneo* is based on classical mythology, and the drama depends on the intervention of a 'real' deity, the sea god Poseidon (Neptune); yet it is a richly human drama, not an allegory, and it makes abundant use of ballet, chorus, and scenic effects.

The character of *Idomeneo* is partly explained by German preoccupation with French culture, though not, except marginally, with French music (see chapters 4 and 5). *Idomeneo* also possesses an immediacy of impact deriving from the circumstances of its commission, for performance by particular artists (see chapters 2 and 3). The poet gives to airy nothing a local habitation and a

1

name; the dramatist, Shakespeare might have added, gives to local talent and its limitations a universal significance. *Idomeneo* is what it is, at least in form, because it was commissioned by Munich, not Milan. The historian cannot, of course, account for Mozart's genius, which turned the ingredients of a serious entertainment into a masterpiece. Nor can the critic or analyst; but close readings of certain sections may provide some evidence for the critical judgement just now implied.

Sources: editions and references

The autograph score of *Idomeneo* was for long kept in its entirety in the Prussian State Library in Berlin. Since the Second World War it has been divided, Act III remains in Berlin while Acts I and II, long considered lost, are now in the Biblioteka Jagiellońska, Kraków. The Bayerische Staatsbibliothek, Munich, possesses the score and performing material used in the 1781 performances. Two librettos were printed in 1781, the first with virtually the whole text as Varesco wrote it and a German translation by J. A. Schachtner, the Salzburg trumpeter and librettist of *Zaide*. The second was available to the Munich audience: hastily produced, it contains a mass of misprints, and yet it does not exactly reflect the probable contents of the first performance (see chapters 1 and 2). Nevertheless, it is a revealing document, close to the actual production, as the first libretto was not.

The only modern edition of the full score is the *Neue Mozart Ausgabe* (henceforth *NMA*; the exact place is II: 5/11), edited by Daniel Heartz (Bärenreiter, 1973). The old Mozart edition (*Mozarts Werke*: henceforth *MW*) is reprinted as a miniature score (No. 417) by Kalmus, and retains its usefulness. These editions were based on divergent editorial policies. *MW* followed the (then extant) autograph, ignoring the cuts entered during the rehearsal period, and thus aimed to represent the original grand plan rather than any actual performance; revisions are included at the end. The main text of *NMA* attempted to reconstruct Mozart's last decisions of 1781 and his 1786 version, presented as alternatives: it thus relegated many original thoughts to an appendix. Unfortunately the autograph material now in Kraków and some of the Munich materials were not available to the *NMA*; a new edition of the 1781 *Idomeneo* is highly desirable. *NMA* is the only score which can be fully relied upon for the 1786 version; it is also available as a vocal score.

Much of our knowledge about *Idomeneo* is derived from the exchange of letters by Wolfgang and Leopold Mozart between November 1780 and January 1781. Because Leopold reached Munich before the première, the letters do not say the final word on what Mozart preferred, or what was actually performed (see chapter 2). But it seems safe to say that, although *Idomeneo* is a work of remarkably certain aim on the part of its composer, it is also a work without a definitive form. The *raison d'être* of this book, however, is that this uncertainty enriches rather than impoverishes our response.

References to the letters are given by date, so that they may be found in any edition to which the reader has access: the bibliography lists the standard editions in English (Anderson) and German (Bauer and Deutsch). Other references in the text and notes are kept to an abbreviated form if the work referred to is listed in the bibliography.

1 Synopsis

The 'argument'

The *argomento* in the printed libretto conveys Varesco's idea of the essential content of the drama. The following translation is nearly literal, but breaks up Varesco's interminable sentences.[1]

Idomeneo, King of Crete, was among the most celebrated heroes who dealt the last death-blow to famous Troy. Returning by sea in glory to his own kingdom, he was overtaken, quite near the port of Sidon, by such a powerful storm that, overcome with terror, he vowed to Neptune that he would sacrifice whatever man he should meet first after reaching shore, if only he and his men were allowed to survive the imminent shipwreck. His son Idamante, wrongly informed of the death of his beloved father, ran to the coast, inconsolable, but perhaps hoping to find some happier news there; by mishap he was the first to meet his father, who, his prayer having been answered by the Sea God, was wandering alone awaiting the promised victim.

The long absence of Idomeneo from his native land, where he had left his son a mere child, meant that neither recognised the other until after an extended conversation.

Idamante loved Princess Ilia, daughter of Priam, King of Troy, whom by courageous action he had saved from a fierce storm when she was arriving, a prisoner, in Crete; she in turn tenderly loved him.[2]

Princess Elettra, daughter of Agamemnon, King of Argos, was a refugee in Crete because of the tragic events in her homeland; she was in love with Idamante, but he did not return her love.

The confused emotions awakened in father and son following their mutual recognition; the paternal love of Idomeneo; his duty towards Neptune; the unhappy condition of Idamante (unaware of his fate); the mutual affection of the lovers, terribly embittered when Idomeneo was constrained to disclose his secret and carry out his cruel vow; the jealousy and desperation of Elettra: all this forms the action of the present drama. The rest will be revealed on stage.

This you may read in the French tragedy, which the Italian poet has imitated in part, changing the tragic into a happy ending.[3]

4

Key to the synopsis:

Numbers and titles of movements: Where numbers differ between editions they appear thus: *NMA* (*Neue Mozart Ausgabe*)/*MW* (*Mozarts Werke*) (see introduction, p. 2, above).

Recitatives: Unless numbered separately, recitatives take the number of the next measured piece: R. 1 is the recitative preceding No. 1. Semp.: semplice (simple, or 'secco') recitative. Obbl.: obbligato (orchestrated, or 'accompagnato', recitative).

Recitative is semplice and measured pieces are arias, unless otherwise indicated. A new bar-count in *NMA* is indicated '*NMA* b. 1'. Criteria for defining aria forms are discussed in chapter 7. The motives mentioned in the synopsis are discussed in chapter 10.

The overture

I make no apology for introducing my synopsis with a full account of the overture: this is, after all, *dramma per musica*, and this overture is surely meant to be heard dramatically, a view supported less by historic considerations than by internal evidence of its structure and its relationship with the rest of the opera.

The overture is an unusual type of sonata form. Nearly half its 164 bars are exposition, modulating to and cadencing in the dominant. Before *Don Giovanni* Mozart seldom offered a substantial development in an overture, and here there is only a retransition, an extended dominant with horn pedal (bars 81–92); from the reprise everything lies within the ambience of the tonic. But Mozart's strategy is subtler than this broad outline suggests. His first mighty paragraph extends to bar 23, but its heterogeneous elements are held together by delay in reaching a cadence. The unison arpeggio (Ex. 1.1, motive A), in which natural brass and (as far as possible) timpani join, is strengthened by the quasi-glissando upbeats of 'French overture' style. The associations of such a musical image fall within the limits set by terms like 'ceremonial', 'authoritative', 'majestic', and, since the rhythm suggests a march, 'military'.[4] From the seventh bar, piano and a flux of crescendo and sforzandi replace the constant fortissimo. From unison the texture becomes a complex continuum (violin tremolando, sustained horns) binding two motives stretched across three octaves, on strings (Ex. 1.1, motive B) and woodwind (motive C). Bars 1 to 6 use every note of the D major scale, but no other, with agogic and metrical emphasis on the triad. The winding string figure (B) introduces three chromatic pitches, one repeated enharmonically (A♯/B♭, bars 9 and 13). Motive B uses even values, motive C distinctively uneven ones (a long note followed by a swift descent) until its repeated last note.[5]

Example 1.1

The impact of such contrast is, in an obvious sense, dramatic: it suggests opposition between authority and forces inimical to it. Mozart may be offering his audience a sign of the kind of drama it is about to witness, following Gluck's prescription (see chapter 4). The next few bars (from 13) show growing homogeneity of texture. The only clear motivic shape is restored to the violins, while the bass attains the dominant (A in bar 19) by a pincer-like movement from B♭ and G♯. The key is implicitly D minor, the style 'Sturm und Drang', until the cessation of harmonic flux (from the dominant, bar 19) is marked by sizzling tremolando scales.[6]

The second paragraph restores the majesty of the opening in a prolonged tutti, a faster arpeggio (basses, bar 23) alternating with violin scales: slow harmonic movement is balanced by surface activity. At bar 23 a sudden shift is made to another comparatively stable plane – the dominant of A – marked by a new motive (Ex. 1.2a); after six bars, this resolves into A major, and pounding rhythms (Ex.1.2b) suggest incipient closure. A textural interruption (bar 41) only serves to reinforce this impression by its cadenza-like preparation for a cadence complete with trill.

Mozart might, at this point, have begun a development, or introduced new material reinforcing the dominant (as at corresponding points in *Don Giovanni* and *La clemenza di Tito*). Instead, A major

Example 1.2

is questioned by its parallel minor, and by a new idea (Ex. 1.3) which owes only its opening turn to Ex. 1.2. Characterised by reverse dotted (Lombard) rhythm, this gracious melody climaxes in a brief lyrical digression to C major (from bar 56), before ending on the dominant (bar 63). A further tutti (using Ex. 1.2b) brings a second quasi-cadenza and a lyrical cadence (bars 78–81), fulfilling earlier expectations of closure; thus Ex. 1.3 has the character of a parenthesis.

Example 1.3

The retransition brings a harsh juxtaposition of motives B and C, the A♯ against A♮ (bar 83) heralding similar clashes in the opera itself. Motive C leads by a bold unison into the reprise. This is literal as far as the plunge into the dominant region (bar 121: cf. bar 29), cancelled six bars later. Neither the cadenza-like descent nor Ex. 1.3 appear where, in a sonata recapitulation, they 'should'.[7] Whereas motives A and C return unmistakably during the opera, and the expressive force of motive B inheres in other chromatic shapes, Ex. 1.3 never resurfaces; the Lombard rhythm, in particular, is not characteristic of *Idomeneo*. Mozart wrote the overture last; perhaps he intended the lyrical melody to prepare the audience for the appearance of Ilia, with whom it has been associated.[8]

Harmonically, Mozart matches the omitted material in the dominant minor with a coda largely in the tonic minor (from bar 137), which quite overcomes the prevailing majestic topos restored at the reprise. Over a dominant pedal, motive C enters with frequently dissonant attack (woodwind), counterpointed to a leaping and sighing string figure, its forte-piano contradicting the normal association of high/loud: low/soft. The passage is repeated over a tonic pedal which by association with the previous passage, and through the persistent E♭s, comes to sound like a dominant; the excruciating E♭/C♯ over D (bar 157) implies an imperfect cadence in G minor. The closing inflection of the bass (C♯-D) and the fading into silence with two significant new motives (D and E, Ex. 1.4) hardly efface this impression, and G minor is indeed the key of the first scene.

Example 1.4

The overture establishes a language of complex interplay of musical character, defined by texture, motive and association, supported by an equivalent harmonic ambiguity. It is hardly possible to trace the complete network of events which may have contributed to the impulse to compose such an introduction. But some attempt will be made; for part of the abiding fascination of *Idomeneo* is the tension between conventional forms and a radical form of continuity.

Act I

SCENE I   *A gallery in the royal palace, leading to various apartments intended for Ilia*

R. I (moving between semp. and obbl.: 'Quando avran fine omai l'aspre sventure mie?' ('When will my bitter misfortunes come to an end?')). Orphaned and exiled, Ilia contemplates her plight. Her inner conflict between loyalty to Troy, hatred of Greece, the desire for revenge, and love for Idamante, appears in the orchestra's heaving syncopations (bar 27) and a richly expressive Adagio (bar 34). A marked cadence in B♭ is settled by an oscillating dotted rhythm (Ex. 1.5, motive F). She invokes 'sweet death'; then impotent fury at the thought of Elettra (whom she assumes Idamante will marry) brings a fierce ascending arpeggio (bar 51), answered by its inversion in the bass. The final cadence melts into the aria. **No. 1** (binary aria, G minor: 'Padre, germani, addio!' (see Ex. 3.3 and chapter 8)). Ilia bids farewell to her family and homeland: Greece is her prison; shall she betray them and love a Greek? But she cannot hate Idamante (motive C). The aria ends equivocally as the cadence plunges into **R. 2** by a descending scale over the traditional suffering interval of a diminished fourth (Ex. 1.6, motive G). Ilia trembles at Idamante's approach.

Example 1.5

Example 1.6

SCENE 2 **R. 2b** (*NMA* b.1). Although very much in control, the young prince is nervous before Ilia. Idomeneo's return is anticipated; Ilia (motive G) contrasts the Greeks, protected by Minerva, with divine victimisation of Troy. Idamante intends to free the Trojan captives; with gallant rhetoric, he declares himself captive to Ilia's beauty. She spurns him with dignity ('Remember, Idamante, who is your father, and who was mine'). The poignancy of the

exchange is underlined when the recitative is disturbed by chromatic harmony and sudden bass activity (Ex. 1.7), clear images of anxiety and pain.

Example 1.7

R. 2

No. 2 (aria, introduction and sonata form, B♭: 'Non ho colpa, e mi condanni'). Idamante feels condemned merely for loving Ilia. Brilliant in style, his aria nevertheless embodies a stance of injured innocence, defined in the sturdy unison opening (Adagio), which forms part of the conversation; there is no ritornello. Declamation turns into lyricism over a complex orchestral continuum, chromatically embittered (bars 2–3) before the gentler cadence.[9] In the Allegro ('Colpa è vostra, oh Dei tiranni') he blames the gods for his misery. A brisk gesture is answered by a shuddering wind figure, and the music plunges into the minor before moving to the dominant. The second strophe of text is introduced by motive C as he makes a more personal approach: if Ilia speaks what he reads in her eyes, he must kill himself. The previous Adagio text is repeated in a middle section (bars 70–86) which forms an extended dominant preparation (nearly all on a pedal F), and derives intensity from an allusion to the overture: a dynamic arpeggio (bar 73; cf. Ex. 1a) is followed by chromatic embellishment of a dominant pedal (cf. bar 137). R. 3 Ilia is spared having to reply by the entry of the Trojans, whom (SCENE 3) Idamante frees in the interests of peace and friendship. Cretans and Trojans (No. 3, chorus with solos from each race, G: 'Godiam la pace') anticipate an era of peace, their emphatic cheerfulness a foil to the alarms which follow.

SCENE 4   **R. 4** Inflamed by jealousy, Elettra reproves Idamante for freeing their enemies; he rebuts her calmly. SCENE 5 (motive G). A sombre Arbace brings the news of the king's shipwreck (obbl.: *NMA* b.1). Distracted, Idamante rushes out. (Semp.) Ilia is moved to pity. As she leaves, the orchestra covers the B minor cadence with a sizzling motive evoking Elettra's jealous fury. SCENE 6 (obbl.: 'Estinto è Idomeneo?'). The motive is repeated a tone lower, a procedure prophetic of the aria to come. To a variant of motive A (bar 36) Elettra avers that Idomeneo's death ends her hope. Idamante will govern the kingdom and himself; (Larghetto) she cannot tolerate a 'slave' winning her hero's heart. (Allegro) A chromatic ascent (from bar 52) breaks into a flood of febrile emotion, reaching a cadence elided with the aria. **No. 4** (binary aria, D minor: 'Tutte nel cor vi sento' (see chapter 11)). Insanely jealous, she is gripped by the Furies of the underworld and vows revenge on Ilia and Idamante alike.

The storm in Elettra's brain becomes the real storm at sea; despite the scene-change the music drives from D minor to C minor without change of tempo. Tremolando texture (motive D) and the vehement motive H (Ex. 9.6a) link the scenes indissolubly.

SCENE 7 *The rocky shore of a rough sea, strewn with wreckage*

No. 5 (binary, C minor: 'Pietà! Numi, pietà'). In the double chorus of drowning sailors and watchers on shore, echo effects match the turbulent alternation of piano and forte in the orchestra (four horns are retained from Elettra's aria). At the reprise (bar 36), SCENE 8, 'Pantomime': 'Neptune appears above the sea. He subdues the violent winds; the sea grows calm. Idomeneo, perceiving him, implores his mercy. Neptune turns a menacing glance on him, then disappears beneath the waves.'[10] Idomeneo lands, and the orchestral *calmando* (motive C) ends over 200 bars of continuous music, one of Mozart's closest approaches to nineteenth-century symphonic opera.[11]

SCENE 9   **R. 6** Idomeneo dismisses his followers; he must be alone to reflect on his vow. An isolated orchestral Andante is picked up by his next words ('Tranquillo è il mar'); he contrasts the calm sea with his own inner agitation. (Obbl.) His vow was insane, cruel; he calls on the gods to release him.[12] **No. 6** (two sections, C major: 'Vedrommi intorno'). This moving aria eschews the florid style for which the first singer, Anton Raaff, was famous; the long notes and the few runs are charged with expression. Much of it is really in C minor, and, exceptionally for an aria, Mozart uses the entire woodwind section. The Andantino uses two strophes of text. The opening fall to the subdominant over a pedal suggests Idomeneo's flagging spirits; the corresponding rise is gently echoed by clarinets. He imagines the ghost of his innocent victim accusing him, and the music explores the tonic minor before moving towards the dominant, marked first by a long note (bar 21, at 'sono innocente') and motive C (bar 27: 'Nel sen trafitto' ('his bosom pierced'). The Allegro di molto requires a third strophe of text. Idomeneo's frenzied grief is underlined by a mournful falling response from the woodwind (bar 60).

As the cadence settles, he sees his victim approach, the orchestra suggesting his horrified reaction. SCENE 10 R. 7 Idamante enters, his characteristic tonality (B♭) interrupting a potential cadence in D, and approaches the stranger on the shore to offer comfort and seek news. Recognition is almost unbearably slow, the dialogue punctured by asides.[13] It emerges that the boy has lost his father. The older man sighs; Idamante asks if he knew Idomeneo. The king does not identify himself but seeks a reason for the boy's interest. As Idamante says 'He is my father' the orchestra initiates a violent Presto (obbl., *NMA* b.1). Every gesture, including winding chromaticism (motive D), mirrors Idamante's comprehension, near disbelief, and impulsive joy. Idomeneo rejects his embrace and rushes off, forbidding his son to follow (an oracular wind-dominated Andante in C minor, bar 27). Idamante's heart is frozen (bar 32: a figure inverting motive H screams in the woodwind); he has infuriated his father, and been rejected without knowing why (motive D again, bar 41). **No. 7** (binary aria, F: 'Il padre adorato'). Perplexity and despair motivate this declamatory piece; the initial rushing semiquavers halt abruptly as he realises his loss (bar 5), and resume (bar 9, and after the pause, bar 14), evoking memories of the recent storm. Although more restrained, as befits Idamante, this aria echoes Elettra's by sinking from D minor to C minor, and reveals a family likeness to Idomeneo's (No. 6) in its last motive, for woodwind in C minor.[14]

INTERMEZZO The sea is calm; the Cretan warriors disembark. The women of Crete run to embrace them. **No. 8** March, during the disembarkation (D: the pompous arpeggios are related to motive A;

motive H appears in bar 9 and motive C in bar 41). **No. 8a** Dance of Cretan women (Gavotte in G, opening with motive C).[15] **No. 9** (chorus, D: 'Nettuno s'onori'). Subtitled 'Ciaccona', this extended movement in honour of the god is sung and danced by Cretan warriors and women; it is riddled with derivatives of motives A and C, which may be intended to underline the irony of so much rejoicing when the audience is well aware of the dramatic situation.[16]

Act II

SCENE 1 *Royal apartments*

1781 (*NMA* **No. 10a**, recitative and aria).

R. 10 Idomeneo explains his vow to Arbace, who advises him to send Idamante abroad, concealing the truth from the Cretans. Idomeneo resolves to send his son to Argos as escort (and perhaps husband) to Elettra.[17] Ilia is seen approaching.

(*MW* **No. 10**; sonata-form aria, C: 'Se il tuo duol'). Arbace's vigorous Allegro bears a simple moral: anguish will always tarnish the splendour of a throne. Of martial character, with brilliant leaps and runs, the aria provides a superfluous foil to what follows; it is usually omitted.

1786 (*NMA* **No. 10b** (recitative (obbl.) and aria, K. 490).

R. 10b Ilia tells Idamante that she knows he loves Elettra, and asks him to remember her kindly. Justly upset by this misrepresentation ('Ch' io mi scordi di te?' ('that I should remember you?') Idamante, believing himself doomed, sings an aria with obbligato violin (Rondo, B♭: 'Non temer, amato bene'); swearing she is his first and only love.[18]

In 1786, a completely new scene replaced the original Act II, scene 1. SCENE 2 **R. 11** Ilia formally congratulates Crete and its king on his escape. Idomeneo hopes the 'principessa gentil' will forget her sorrows. She replies enigmatically that bitterness has borne sweet fruit.[19] **No. 11** (binary aria, E♭: 'Se il padre perdei'). Muted strings begin a six-bar phrase whose half-close is covered by the solo flute, leading four obbligato winds (flute, oboe, bassoon, horn) in an answering period drawn out to nine bars. This music is repeated for 'If I have lost my father, you will be father to me'. The new motive at bar 27 ('Crete is now my loving home') has been associated with motive C.[20] Ilia's floating vocal line has more than a touch of minor colour: Mozart intimates that she is too sensitive to, as she claims, 'no longer recall the anguish and pain'. The closing lines ('Now heaven offers joy and contentment to repay my distress') bring the voice into closer rapport with the wind. After a two-bar link the music is symmetrically recapitulated, with an extended cadence; such are the bald facts of an aria in which Mozart exploited the skills of his singer and players without imperilling Ilia's tragic serenity (see chapter 7).

SCENE 3 **R. 12** (obbl.) Ilia leaves the king in turmoil. His recitative exploits fragments from her aria, for he understands what she leaves unsaid, realising that Neptune will claim three victims: Idamante as sacrifice, Ilia and himself from broken hearts. Indeed, he wonders if it is not Idamante's kindness to the Trojans which has caused Neptune to punish the boy. **No. 12** (sonata, D: 'Fuor del mar'). Escaping from the sea, he has found a more furious tempest at home; why does threatening Neptune delay his destruction, when his heart is so close to shipwreck? The magnificently surging music, which uses trumpets and drums for the first time in Act II, is enhanced in the original version (**No. 12a**) by splendid coloratura designed to display Raaff's accomplishments without exhausting him: it is thus more in line with the capabilities of modern singers than most *opera seria* display arias. Nevertheless in 1786 Mozart prepared a shorter, simpler version (**No. 12b**; see chapter 8).

SCENE 4 (1781). Idomeneo meets Elettra, who thanks him for courteously providing an escort.[21] In 1786 this dialogue is omitted; the cadence of **No. 12b** is covered by rhythmic momentum and a modulation for Elettra's entrance (*NMA* p. 269; *MW* p. 348).
SCENE 5 (1786 Scene 4) **R. 13** (obbl.). Elettra expresses confidence that, away from her rival, Idamante can be induced to love her. The recitative is mainly based on the second theme from No. 13. **No. 13** (binary aria, G: 'Idol mio'). The strings-only orchestration is a symptom of the extreme contrast between this and Elettra's other arias. She reflects that a love not easily won is the more charming, and that proximity brings affection. The melody is seductively tender; the second quatrain, in the dominant (bar 30), makes a delicate thematic point in the reprise (bar 94) where it is inverted to its 'original' form as a variant of motive C. The cadence elides with **No. 14** (March, C), which starts with wind instruments,

another, purely theatrical, reason for using only strings in No. 13. Brass and upper strings are muted, the timpani covered. In a striking anticipation of a favourite nineteenth-century device, Elettra's recitative is superimposed on the March, which summons her to embark and covers the change of scene. At its last reprise, Mozart directs the mutes to come off while the whole orchestra makes a crescendo to fortissimo.

SCENE 6 *Port of Sidon with ships lining the shore*

R. 15 Elettra forgives Crete the sorrow her visit has brought her. No. 15 (chorus with solo, E: 'Placido è il mar, andiamo') is an enchanting picture of a calm sea and the prospect of a happy voyage. Elettra begs for kindly Zephyr breezes; as if heeding her prayer, woodwinds (bar 44) restore the tonic for the repeat of the chorus. SCENE 7 A brusque gesture covers the cadence as Idomeneo enters with Idamante. R. 16 The king orders his reluctant son to embark; he must perform a thousand heroic deeds and become worthy of kingship by helping the unfortunate (initially the orphaned Elettra). No. 16 (Trio, F: 'Pria di partir, oh Dio?')[22] Idamante begs to kiss his father's hand; Elettra makes a more ornate farewell. Idomeneo wishes her happiness, but the orchestra (bar 25) marks his inner agitation as he tells his son to accept his fate. Idomeneo's prayer (bar 28, 'Seconda i voti, oh ciel') is taken up by the others in a richly elaborated cadence; Idamante's heart will remain in Crete. A chromatic lament from the violins (bar 49) is followed by an ascending figure reminiscent of the end of the overture, accompanying the inarticulate farewells of father and son; even Elettra is worried ('O dei! che sara?'). The three unite, in a faster tempo, to implore the clemency of heaven, but as they prepare to embark, the cadence is rudely shattered by a storm, awesomely depicted in No. 17 (chorus: più allegro, F minor: 'Qual nuovo terrore'). The waters swell, the heavens roar, lightning burns the ships, and a huge monster rises from the sea.

Here the drama takes on a wider dimension; the fate of the people of Crete, not just its rulers, hangs in the balance. Significantly, the musical style, and one harmonic trait (modulation down a tone: at bar 32 B♭ minor after preparation for C minor), recall Elettra's first aria (No. 4) as well as the storm chorus (No. 5). The people are assailed by Mozart's powerful orchestral and harmonic invention. If the heavens are angry, someone is to blame: three times they cry 'Il reo, qual'è?' ('The sinner, who is he?'). Motive H is in the violins, and the harmony grinds enharmonically downwards, again by whole tones: B♭ minor, G♯ minor, F♯ minor. Each cry ends in a pause on a diminished seventh. These sequential descents, their disruptive power apparent to the most untutored ear, use all the three available positions of the diminished seventh, approaching the edge of harmonic comprehensibility in eighteenth-century terms, like the statue music in *Don Giovanni*. The principal tonality of the chorus, C minor, is never restored. This is no place for stability or reconciliation; only the dominant of B♭ minor acts as temporary repose.

The key is wrenched towards D major as Idomeneo finds his voice: 'Eccoti in me, barbaro Nume, il reo!' (obbl., *NMA* b.1). He addresses the gods, but his awestruck people overhear his confession. Amid orchestral upheavals more regal than stormy, he demands that the gods should punish only him; there must be no innocent second victim (at bar 19 a melting woodwind figure suggests motive C; the tempo slows to Adagio). If the gods insist, they forfeit their claim to be called just. For such a significant speech, the recitative is extremely compressed, perhaps on Mozart's insistence.[23] **No. 18** (chorus, D minor: 'Corriamo, fuggiamo'). The storm rages on; the Cretans, appalled by the guilty king's blasphemous defiance, flee in confusion. The movement is a dark cousin of the overture, employing motives A, C and E (see Ex. 1.8), the latter enhancing the pianissimo end of a terror-struck diminuendo.[24]

Example 1.8

No. 18

a.   Cor - ria - mo, fug - gia - mo quel mo - stro spie - ta - to!

Act III

SCENE 1 *A royal garden*

R. 19 (obbl.) Ilia is unaware of these violent happenings, and this scene forms a brief idyll before the crisis. She has lost Idamante, but his departure lifts an intolerable burden of conflicting loyalties. She confides to the garden air the cost of suppressing her love. In the short recitative sustained strings have only one motivic shape, a gentle echo of the final cadence to Act II which anticipates the opening of the aria. **No. 19** (sonata-form aria, E: 'Zeffiretti lusinghieri'). The orchestration is softened by resting the oboes; fluttering violins gently evoke the Zephyr. A gentle exchange between woodwind and voice (bar 30) defines the dominant key-area, as she begs the winds to bear her love to Idamante. The middle section is centred on the tonic minor; she waters the garden with tears shed for the fragility of love. The approach to the reprise is stressful with dissonance, chromaticism, and wide melodic intervals (see Ex. 9.1). The final cadence is again elided with the recitative. **R. 20a** (obbl.) The orchestra suggests Ilia's violent agitation at the unexpected apparition of Idamante; should she escape or stay?

SCENE 2 **R. 20b** (semp.) Idamante requests a single word before going to his death – she can only echo him: 'Morir? tu, prence?'– he must kill the monster or die in the attempt. Her concern leads her to admit that she loves him. (Obbl., *NMA* b.1) The flow of violin semiquavers turns his declamation into arioso; her revelation fills him with wonder. Supported by a dignified dotted figure, she explains that family pride, which caused her coldness, has died in the face of his danger. She, too, develops her thought in an arioso, blended with the gracious opening of the following duet, which represents complete harmony between them. **No. 20a** (1781: two movements, A: 'S'io non moro a questi accenti'). In the Andante Ilia responds to Idamante's declaration with real passion, driving the tonality towards remote C major. He asks her to be his wife: her 'Lo sposo mio sarai tu' ('You will be my husband') brings motive C. In the Allegretto the lightest possible time-signature ($\frac{3}{8}$) and luxuriant doubling in thirds anticipate *Così fan tutte*. This duet was omitted in 1781, but in 1786 Mozart composed a replacement, in the same key, **No. 20b** ('Spiegarti non poss' io', K. 489). It is prefaced by the same figure as No. 20a, and motive C reappears when Ilia admits her love (bar 8). This single-movement duet (which should always be performed when Idamante is a tenor) is more conventional in sentiment than the original Andante, and more florid; only a chromatic upbeat (bar 34) replaces the expressive modulations of No. 20a. But it is more concise; the drama is less completely forgotten than in the $\frac{3}{8}$ Allegretto.[25]

SCENE 3 **R. 21** (obbl.) The duet is barely ended when the lovers are surprised by Idomeneo, disturbed to find his fears confirmed, and an indignant Elettra. (Semp.) Strengthened by love, Idamante boldly asks his father how he has offended. The king is evasive: Neptune's hatred has frozen his natural affection. Idamante wonders if the fault is his own; Idomeneo tells his son to find a distant haven; Ilia entreats Elettra's comfort, to the muttered annoyance of that spurned princess. (Obbl.) Idamante, over a heart-stopping modulation ('Oh Ilia, Oh genitor'), bids Ilia not to follow him but to live in peace. **No. 21** Quartet (binary, E♭: 'Andrò ramingo e solo'). Mozart recomposed the voice parts with great care for a tenor Idamante; the two versions are superimposed in *NMA*.[26] The descending unison and its chromatic response (compare the beginning of the overture) are repeated and developed in Idamante's opening line, the long low E♭ an image of a young man staring despair in the face (Ex. 1.9). Ilia, with more overt passion, demands to be his companion in sorrow and death. Idomeneo exclaims that Neptune is merciless in not ending his life. In a growth of musical density, Elettra closely imitates Idomeneo's music: 'When shall I have revenge?' – an equally futile plea. Although the ensemble is static in that the action is unaffected, the music of the quartet effects mercurial changes in mood, and the drama is developed by the quality of its insight into the minds of the principals. The lovers beg Idomeneo to calm his anger (sweet thirds, bar 35); but all three have broken hearts (jagged rhythmic unison). The four unite at 'Soffrir più non si può . . .' ('I can no longer bear such sorrow, worse than death. None has ever suffered a crueller fate, a harsher punishment'). In a remarkable denial of musical decorum, the central cadence is in B♭ *minor* (bar 67), already hinted at by Ilia's first phrase. The second part, repeating all the text, is no simple recapitulation; it intensifies what is already almost unbearable. Idamante's melody is distorted and overlaid by Ilia, who thrusts the key upwards ('io morirò': her positive determination to die with Idamante); the next sequence

declines inexorably from Idomeneo's angry 'Nettun spietato!' and
Elettra's cry for revenge, now more fully expressed (bars 89–92).
From bar 92 the reprise is more exact, but the closing section is
prolonged as if in desperation; expression of foreboding postpones
its inevitable fulfilment. Mozart extends the coda (using C♭ major,
130), the voices harrowingly intertwined; for all their differences
they are at one in their fear for Idamante. The E♭ minor cadences
bring motive C three times (bar 148–53). But the singers cannot
cadence: after a dominant pause, three fall silent, and Idamante
repeats his first phrase without its answering resolution. As he
leaves, the orchestra reaches a standstill alone, its last bars gently
animated by motive F.

Example 1.9

No. 21

SCENE 4 **R. 22a** Arbace announces that the High Priest of
Neptune, speaking for the people, demands to see the king. Idomeneo
knows all is lost. SCENE 5 **R. 22b** (obbl.: 'Sventurata Sidon!').
Arbace cannot affect the action, nor is his fate of interest; but this
recitative is an unforgettable image of desolation, and a bridge
between, and relief from, the intimate and public dramas.[27] It begins
with a troubled sequence strangely closing on motive F, which was
most recently associated with Ilia.[28] Arbace meditates on the city of
tears, the realm of mourning. Looking to heaven he spies a gleam of
hope, to music of daring fragility; he is quickly disappointed (motive
G, bar 25). Sweeping allegro figures foretell a tragic ending. **No. 22**
(sonata, A: 'Se colà ne'fati è scritto'). Although using only strings,
this is more warmly expressive than Arbace's first aria, but it also

bows to *opera seria* in its cadential floridity. He offers his own life as a sacrifice, begging for mercy towards the kingdom and its princes.

SCENE 6 *A grand square with statues, the façade of the palace to one side. Idomeneo enters accompanied by Arbace and a royal train; the king supported by Arbace seats himself on the throne intended for public audiences; High Priest and many people*

No. 23 (recitative obbl.). A short, imposing march (motive A) precedes an enigmatic allusion to motive E (bar 8), harshly suppressed by stormy images (bar 10); then a powerful arpeggio, symbol of authority, descends from the violins to the basses (strengthened by woodwind).[29] Only the High Priest dare accuse the king on behalf of his suffering people: 'Behold, Sire, the devastation all around; blood, bodies swollen with black poison, thousands swallowed alive by the insatiable monster.' More calmly, the priest reminds the king that he alone has the remedy. With a powerful flourish (motive A) he urges him: 'To the temple, Sire: Who, where, is the victim?' From unison, the strings split into wild imitation as the king's resistance crumbles. Tremolo supported by hollow-sounding low wind (bar 75), then a sequence on motive C (melded with G), accompany Idomeneo's halting admission that 'the victim is Idamante': then motive C pours down (bar 83), inextricably entwined with motive D, a potent image of draining hope. **No. 24** (chorus with solo; C minor: 'Oh voto tremendo'). This display of public emotion matches Mozart's greatest sacred music: 'O terrible vow! O horrible sight! Death reigns over us and has opened up the cruel abyss.' The chorus breaks in at the top of a slow chromatic ascent, imitated in the second phrase by the wind, a suppressed cry of nature outraged. The priest asks heaven to spare the innocent. The exact choral repeat marks a move into ritual mode; but as the people sorrowfully depart, a coda in C major – is it hope or the serenity of despair? – anticipates the highest pathos of Beethoven. More mundanely it prepares the key of the following number. **No. 25** The march (F, two repeated sections) moves definitively into ritual, and also covers the change of scene.[30]

SCENE 7 *The great hall of the temple of Neptune, filling with people below and in the galleries. The sea is visible in the distance. Priests are seen preparing the sacrifice. Idomeneo enters with a numerous and magnificent train.*

No. 26 (binary cavatina with chorus, F: 'Accogli, oh re del mar'). Idomeneo's private feelings are subsumed in the collective, ritual solution to the nation's agony; the impersonal nature of his utterance is prepared by the introduction, in which a solemn woodwind melody is accompanied by a filigree of pizzicato strings. Idomeneo's prayer is lyrical; penitence should win mercy and calm the seas. Twice the priests respond with a chillingly hieratic monotone, sombrely harmonised. The mood is shattered by a brusque D major fanfare and cries of 'victory' from off-stage. SCENE 8 **R. 27** Arbace announces that Idamante, risking his life, has killed the monster. Idomeneo fears that such sacrilege will increase Neptune's wrath, so that Idamante must still die.

SCENE 9 **Recitative** (obbl.: *NMA* **No. 27**; *MW* no number. 'Padre, mio caro padre'). An expressive Largo in A♭ major (Ex. 1.10) brings Idamante robed in white, garlanded for sacrifice, surrounded by guards and priests. He offers his life to his father with touching simplicity: now he understands; love, not hatred, caused his rejection. A figure in close imitation (bar 16) haloes his exquisite arioso: how fortunate is Idamante that he who gave him life now returns it to the gods (motive C, exquisitely combined with itself in contrary motion). To prepare Idomeneo's reply, a serene phrase in E♭ recalls Ex. 1.10.

Idomeneo asks forgiveness (arioso), matching his son's noble renunciation; but he cannot endure it, and breaks the grip of ritual (furious arpeggios in F minor and D) with a fierce denunciation ('Barbaro, iniquo fato'); who can raise the sacrificial axe against his own child? While remaining controlled, Idamante insists with increased energy that there is no other way: pity and love must not divert sacrifice. To a crisp Andante (bar 58) he recalls his father to duty; the gods' favour will grant him a hundred more sons; anyway, the people are his children. As he thinks of Ilia, the motive of Ex. 1.10 returns, after seventy bars, now in imitation, followed by a drooping version of motive C (bar 75); if she cannot be his wife, let her be his father's daughter. **No. 27** (*MW*: *NMA* 27a; tenary aria, D: 'No, la morte io non pavento').[31] Idamante adopts D major, without the regal panoply of trumpets and drums but with an active arpeggio accompaniment; the aria is part of the dialogue, lacking ritornello or coda. He does not fear death, the price of peace for his father and country, and in the central Larghetto he looks forward to Elysium. After the full reprise, the cadence leaps into recitative: why does his father delay? Idomeneo pulls himself

Example 1.10

No. 27

together for a last embrace (*NMA* bar 88: Largo in D♭, the voices
uniting over a violin continuum). Idamante again remembers Ilia,
SCENE 10 who at the last moment rushes in (Elettra following)
to separate him from the ritual weapon. Idomeneo is abashed;
Idamante and the priest reprove Ilia; she fights her way forward.[32]
Scion of a defeated race, Ilia demands to be the sacrifice herself.
Idamante (arioso, with frantic arpeggio accompaniment) appeals
to her pride: she must live as sole remnant of great Troy. Idomeneo
invokes the gods, but he knows the sacrifice of Ilia will gain nothing.

(Arioso, allegretto) Idamante says his own death will be the ultimate sign of Ilia's love, but she runs to the altar and kneels before the priest. Thunder from below; Neptune's statue moves.

No. 28[33] Trombones proclaim the awful majesty of the sea god. His voice declares that love has triumphed; Idomeneo, having reneged on his vow, must abdicate, but the gods demand no further sacrifice. Idamante will reign with Ilia. *NMA* No. 29 (*MW* no number; recitative obbl.: 'O ciel pietoso!') After the subterranean booming, the high woodwind evoke a clear sky. The general delight is dispelled by Elettra, in a recitative of serpentine fury for which even Act I hardly prepares us.[34] *MW* No. 29 (binary, C minor: 'D'Oreste, d'Ajace'). Her venomous aria was apparently cut before the first performance, but it is too powerful a revelation of her true character, suppressed since Act I, to be omitted with equanimity. The furies and demons exorcised by the oracle have entered her soul, yet their audible hissing (violins) cannot disguise her genuine heartbreak (woodwind echoes, bars 40ff.; motive C at the cadence).

SCENE ULTIMA No. 30 (recitative obbl., E♭, Adagio: 'Popoli, a voi l'ultima legge') This is a fully cadenced number with ritornello, although it ends in the dominant, B♭. Clarinets are the only woodwind, with horns and strings. A gentle motive is taken up in canon, the counterpoint including motive C, the cadence hinting at motive E (see Ex. 12.2); Idomeneo's speech is punctuated by developments of this material. He offers his people one final law; peace follows the completion of the sacrifice: Neptune will favour them, ruled by 'another myself' ('un altro me stesso') and his royal bride. *NMA* No. 30a, *MW* No. 31 (ternary aria, B♭ – a binary Adagio with faster middle section: 'Torna la pace intorno'). Although theatrical pressure caused its omission, Mozart composed Raaff's last aria with loving care.[35] Symbolically, it crowns the drama by using the key formerly associated with Idamante (just as Idamante's last aria adopted 'regal' D major). Peace returns to the king; his old age will be filled with vigour. The sentiments are generalised, but this renunciation is indispensable to the character's progression.

NMA No. 31, *MW* No. 32 (chorus, D: 'Scenda Amor, scenda Imeneo'). Whether or not the last aria is performed, B♭ is succeeded without preamble by brilliant D major, with trumpets and drums. In a brisk allegro, repeated after a dance, the people call on the gods of love and marriage to unite the royal couple. BALLET *NMA* No. 32 (*MW*, separately published: K. 367). The huge Chaconne

(318 bars) begins with the same motive as the previous chorus. It pauses for a Larghetto (bar 154, still in triple time), and resumes (bar 207) in a variety of moods within the main tempo before a grand reprise (bar 284). Ending with a pause on the dominant, the Chaconne is succeeded by a Largo (still in D) for a solo dancer, an Allegretto, and a faster conclusion (a further 160 bars). This feast of uninhibitedly pleasurable music forms a brilliant, courtly spectacle, returning the opera to its origins in *tragédie lyrique* and *opera seria*.[36]

2   Genesis of an operone

STANLEY SADIE

Mozart's connections with the Munich court dated back to just before his sixth birthday, when he was taken there to be exhibited: it was his first venture as a musician, probably his first of any kind, outside his native Salzburg. He was there again the following year, at the beginning of the lengthy tour that was to take him to Paris and London, and once more, on the way back, three and a half years later. The fourth visit was in 1774–5, when his *opera buffa La finta giardiniera* was given at the Salvator Theatre during the carnival season; anxious to make an impression in Munich beyond the opera house, he wrote a number of liturgical works, among them a powerful *Misericordias Domini* (K. 222/205a) in a learned, contrapuntal style.

The years 1777–8 saw Mozart's crucial journey to Mannheim and Paris, seeking career opportunities away from the provincialism and pettiness of Salzburg and its court. Munich was his first important stop. In a letter home to his father (2 October 1777) he fantasised about staying there and earning a living composing operas:

I should draw up a contract with Count Seeau [intendant of the court opera] along the following lines: to compose every year four German operas, some *buffe*, some *serie*, with a benefit night, as is the custom here . . . with my help the German national theatre would certainly be a success. When I heard the German Singspiel I was simply itching to compose.

He added that a German serious opera was in prospect 'and they are very anxious that I should compose it'. A few days later (11 October) he was writing of his 'inexpressible longing' (*'unaussprechliche begierde'*) to write an opera.

The visit to Munich proved fruitless, at least for the moment; so, too, did the much longer visit to Mannheim, where again he was told there was no vacancy. But he took the opportunity to tell the Elector there 'my dearest wish is to write an opera here' (8 November). It could be a German opera, he added, for the

Mannheim court had recently been encouraging opera in the native tongue; while he was there Mozart heard Holzbauer's *Günther von Schwarzburg* (1777) and came to know two operas by Schweitzer, his *Alceste* (1775) and his *Rosamunde* (written by 1778 but not performed until 1780). That, however, was not really the kind of opera he wanted to write himself: 'Don't forget how much I long to write operas', he wrote again (4 February 1778), '. . . but Italian, not German; *seria*, not *buffa*'. And three days later: 'Writing operas is at the forefront of my mind: French rather than German, Italian rather than German or French.' Possibly he would have been invited to write an opera for Mannheim had it not been for what in effect was the elimination of the court as a separate entity when, after the death of the Elector Maximilian III Joseph in Munich, the ruling Elector Palatine Karl Theodor became Elector of Bavaria, and the Mannheim and Munich courts amalgamated. On his return journey from Paris to Salzburg at the turn of the year, 1778–9, Mozart paused at Munich to see his friends from Mannheim and to present the new Electress with a dedication copy of his set of accompanied sonatas, begun the previous autumn in Mannheim and now newly printed in Paris; he stayed on until 12 January to hear the carnival opera, Schweitzer's *Alceste* (Aloysia Weber was singing a minor role).

The 1779–80 carnival opera at Munich was Franz Paul Grua's *Telemaco*. Mozart's opportunity to write one himself was not to be long delayed. He had made good friends among the Mannheim musicians, including the elderly but still influential and admired tenor Anton Raaff, the sopranos Dorothea and Elisabeth Wendling and their husbands, who were members of the orchestra, and Christian Cannabich, *Kapell Director* at the Mannheim court (see chapter 3 below). Raaff and Cannabich in particular may well have spoken in Mozart's favour (he mentions in the letter of 31 December 1778 that they had made great efforts on his behalf) when it came to selecting a composer for the 1781 carnival opera – the most important opera production of the year, at Munich as at virtually all the Catholic courts. But the decision will ultimately have rested with Count Seeau and Karl Theodor himself. Cannabich was a particular friend of Countess Baumgarten, who according to Mozart (letter of 13 November 1780) was a 'favourite' of the Elector.

The commission for *Idomeneo* was presumably negotiated by Count Seeau, during the summer of 1780; no letters survive, nor has any record of the contract come to light in the Munich archives.

The fee Mozart received is unknown. When in the letter from Munich of 2 October 1779 he had referred to composing German operas for the city, he had reckoned 125 gulden for each, or about 28 ducats, no princely sum (the Viennese court opera that season paid fees of 213 and 307 gulden to Ruprecht and Beecke), though there would also have been a benefit night.[1] For a large-scale, serious Italian opera for the carnival he would certainly expect substantially more than that. His librettist received 20 ducats and the German translator 10 ducats. The Viennese practice was for a librettist to be paid about one-third (sometimes less than a quarter, sometimes nearly a half) of the fee allowed to the composer; if the same applied to Munich, Mozart's fee would have been in the region of 60 ducats or 254 gulden. His current annual salary at Salzburg was 450 gulden.

The choice of topic for an opera traditionally lay with the commissioning authority, not with the composer. The previous carnival opera, Grua's *Telemaco*, had as its chief modern source Fénelon's *Aventures de Télémaque* (1699), in which the story of Idomeneus is also related. The choice of librettist must certainly have been made by Mozart and his father. The days when he would simply set a preexisting text as it stood were now passed; for a new opera he needed to work closely with his librettist. Clearly it was advisable to choose a local man as collaborator. The only Italian poet available in Salzburg was Gianbattista Varesco (1735–1805), chaplain to the Archbishop; his name must certainly have been put forward to Seeau by the Mozarts. He was required to prepare an Italian version of the 1712 text by Antoine Danchet for Campra, based on Fénelon and the 1705 drama of Crébillon, but with the *lieto fine* (happy ending) that by this date was obligatory, politically and philosophically.[2] The first version of the text was prepared, and presumably submitted for official approval, in time for Mozart to begin work in the autumn or even the late summer.

Composition

It was the normal practice throughout the eighteenth century for the composer of a major opera to write most of it, in the city where it was to be performed, during the weeks immediately preceding the première. He could work out the opera's broad plan in advance, and probably compose the recitatives, as well as any choruses and ensembles; then, as each singer arrived, he would hear him or her and compose the arias to suit the voice (to 'fit the clothes

exactly to the figure', as Leopold had written of his son's composition of *Mitridate*, 24 November 1770). Mozart, of course, already
knew several of the singers: Raaff, who was to sing Idomeneo;
Dorothea Wendling, Ilia; Elisabeth Wendling, Elettra; Domenico de'
Panzacchi, a court *virtuoso da camera*, Arbace; and almost certainly
he knew Giovanni Valesi, the High Priest. Only Vincenzo dal Prato,
the castrato who was cast as Idamante, was unknown to him. So
he could, if he had wished, have composed the opera, except for
the arias for the *primo uomo*, consecutively from the beginning.

Part of the opera, then, is likely to have been written before
Mozart left Salzburg for Munich on 5 November 1780 (among
those who saw him off, incidentally, was a theatre manager and
performer currently playing in Salzburg, none other than Emanuel
Schikaneder). Happily for posterity, his father did not go with
him: because of their separation – and Leopold's serving as inter-
mediary between composer and librettist (as well as commentator
on the messages he conveyed) – there exists a comprehensive
correspondence between father and son, unique of its kind for the
eighteenth century, which illuminates every aspect of the work's
genesis; its planning, its composition, its staging, the theatrical and
other practical factors affecting its performance, and above all
Mozart's attitudes towards the relationship of the words and the
drama to the music. Leopold joined his son two or three days
before the première, on 29 January; Mozart's last letter was sent
eleven days before, by which time many (though, as we shall see,
probably not all) of the decisions had been made.

Mozart arrived in Munich at 1 p.m. on 6 November, after an
uncomfortable overnight journey, and made contact the next morning with Count Seeau. On 8 November he sent some instructions
to Varesco about the presentation of the libretto for printing. This
letter sounds the first warning that alterations would be needed,
including cuts in the recitative, but there is also an assurance that
the whole of Varesco's text (in which, as we shall see, the poet
evidently took great pride) would be printed in the libretto to be
on sale in the opera house. This was not, in fact, an uncommon
procedure; often quotation marks indicated the passages left unset
('versi virgolati'). There is one specific request, that Varesco should
adjust the text of 'Se il padre perdei' to remove a spoken aside ('*à
parte reden*'). It has sometimes been supposed that Mozart meant
here words literally to be spoken; yet the fact that he says such an
aside would be admissible in dialogue (that is, recitative) but not in

an aria, where words have to be repeated, seems to indicate that what Varesco had specified must have been a normal, sung aside – there is after all no example of a spoken aside in any Mozart work, though asides in recitative style are numerous. A repeated aside, even sung, would indeed be clumsy in a serious aria (as it would not be in an *opera buffa* ensemble, for example); a true spoken aside in an aria is surely unthinkable. Mozart also mentions that 'we have agreed' that this number is to be an Andantino with obbligato flute, oboe, bassoon, and horn. 'We' would seem to be Seeau, Cannabich (the principal conductor), and Mozart, perhaps also Dorothea Wendling herself.

Clearly this aria, which falls early in Act II, had not been composed before Mozart left Salzburg, although Mozart knew Dorothea Wendling's voice well.[3] It is, however, written on paper of a type he had used regularly in Salzburg since 1779. The same type, a ten-stave paper (which would be unsuitable for numbers demanding large forces), is used for the whole of Act I, apart from two of the three choruses (Nos. 5 and 9) and Idomeneo's aria (No. 6, with the preceding recitative); for all of Act II except, again, Idomeneo's aria and the choruses; and in Act III for Ilia's aria (No. 19), the duet (No. 20a) and Arbace's aria (No. 22). It is clearly unsafe to draw firm conclusions on the basis of paper-types about times of composition, partly because it is impossible to be certain of the provenance of some of the papers (another used extensively in *Idomeneo* turns up in Salzburg works, Vienna works and Munich ones, with different stave rulings), and partly because Mozart did not necessarily use paper in discrete batches; moreover, it is clear that he brought Salzburg paper with him to Munich. And sometimes the choice of paper may turn on nothing more than whether an item would fit comfortably on to the normal Salzburg ten-stave format; certainly in Act I the three numbers for which Salzburg paper was not used are the three most fully scored. But paper evidence may sometimes be suggestive, and more than that when it comes to the Vienna version of 1786.

In this first letter, Mozart also tells Leopold the disturbing news he has heard about Dal Prato – his breath gives out in the middle of an aria and (incorrectly) he has never been on the stage before; imagine, he says, with Raaff as stiff as a statue, how the Act I scene will be (he is referring to the recognition scene, which it seems they regarded as crucial). But Dorothea Wendling is 'arcicontentissima' with her scene ('Padre, germani, addio' and the preceding recitative) that opens the opera; he had been required to play it over for her three times (see chapter 3). Leopold responded on 11 November, enclosing a further aria and the completed libretto.

Shaping an 'operone'

By the time of Mozart's next letter, 13 November, serious discussion of the shape of the drama had begun. There are, running through his letters, two recurrent themes: brevity and naturalness. In this one he tells Leopold – who, it is understood, will pass it on to Varesco – that 'the second duet' was to be dropped from the sacrifice scene (during the tussle between Ilia and Idamante over which of them should be the victim),

and indeed with more profit than loss to the opera; for, when you read the scene over, you realise that it becomes limp and cold – and for the other actors, who have to stand around doing nothing, very *gênant*; and besides, the noble struggle between Ilia and Idamante becomes prolonged and loses its force.

On that day Mozart lunched at Seeau's with Cannabich, Lorenzo Quaglio (the designer), and Le Grand (the ballet-master). The responsibility for managing the stage action in opera at this period was not firmly defined. Generally it fell to the librettist, if he was present; the composer might also expect some say. So would the designer and particularly the ballet-master, and indeed a later letter (15 November) makes it clear that the 'action and grouping' had lately been settled with Le Grand. Singers themselves played a considerable part, depending on their status within the cast, in the decisions that bore on the staging of their own arias. Such a division of responsibility, if difficult to reconcile with the attitudes of our own age when a director is expected to impose a unified interpretation of his own, is more readily understood in respect of the eighteenth century, when stage conventions were so highly developed and stage comportment so well understood that there was little scope for disagreement.

It was in fact Quaglio who had raised one important objection which earlier, apparently, had occurred to Mozart and his father; they all queried the propriety of having the king, Idomeneo, alone on the ship on his first entry.

If the Abbé thinks he can be reasonably represented in the terrible storm, forsaken by everyone, *without a ship*, all alone in the greatest danger, so be it: but please note, no ship, as he can't be alone in a ship; if he is, there must be a few trusted generals landing with him. Then he will say a few words to his people and ask them to leave him alone – all quite natural, in his melancholy situation. (13 November)

Leopold expressed his agreement sharply (18 November):

Idomeneo must leave the ship with his retinue. Then come the words he addresses to them, and they withdraw. You remember, I had made this objection to Munich, but they replied that thunderstorms and the sea pay no attention to the laws of etiquette. Yes, indeed, if a shipwreck were to follow. But they are released by the vow. Above all, the landing will produce a splendid effect.

As to the duet, whose title was 'Deh soffri in pace, o cara', Varesco had refused to hear of its being cut, but Leopold reports that he has persuaded him: instead, he says, there should be a short recitative, interrupted by a subterranean rumbling and voice (which, with its accompaniment, must be 'moving, alarming, and extraordinary' as well as 'a masterpiece of harmony'). Leopold goes on to amplify this with more detailed instructions, which Mozart indeed followed, although some of the recitative was later cut. Leopold's other points in this letter are trivial ones (for example, distinguishing between 'Achivo' and 'Argivo' and specifying the accentuation of 'natío'). It is not surprising to see Leopold drawing his son's attention to such points of detail, but more so to find him writing so specifically on ways in which particular passages should be treated. These must have been the habits of many years.

This letter of Leopold's apparently crossed with one of Mozart's (15 November) requiring still more alterations. He has, he writes, been working with Raaff, whose Act I aria does not permit him the cantabile singing he wants and who 'can no longer show off in such an aria as that in Act II – "Fuor del mar"'. (This may seem to imply that Leopold already knew the aria; but in fact it was not composed when Mozart left Salzburg – it is on 'Munich' paper, and Mozart had not yet shown it to Raaff, as he would certainly have done had it been written. Clearly Mozart was alluding to Raaff's capacities in a bravura aria, of the kind this was intended to be, rather than to this one as actually composed.) Raaff now demanded an extra aria at the end of the third act, where it would displace a planned quartet: 'Thus, too, a useless piece will be got rid of – and Act III will be far more effective.' Mozart also proposes to drop a short aria, 'or rather a sort of cavatina', within the Act II finale and substitute a recitative; this is the passage 'Io solo errai', when the thunderstorm has frustrated the departure of Elettra and

Idamante. 'There will be such noise and confusion on the stage that an aria at this moment would cut a feeble figure – and then there is the thunderstorm – which is hardly likely to break off just for Mr Raaff's aria, is it?' Leopold responded (18 November) that it would be altered to a 'spirited recitative, which if necessary may be accompanied with thunder and lightning'. Mozart's letter also includes a complaint about 'my molto amato Castrato dal Prato', who has no idea how to sing an *Eingang* (a 'lead-in', or miniature cadenza) and is going to have to be taught the entire opera, note by note.

During his first two weeks in Munich Mozart, it seems, composed scarcely a note towards his new opera: his time was heavily occupied with necessary social calls, planning meetings, and sessions with the singers. His only composition was a long-promised aria, for which his father was pressing him, for Schikaneder (which he dispatched on 22 November; it is lost). The première, scheduled for 20 January, was a mere two months off. It seems that about half the opera was written by now. Ilia's first aria, Idomeneo's first and probably his second, Elettra's first two (Lisel Wendling had sung them through half a dozen times, and expressed her delight, by the time of Mozart's letter of 15 November) and probably Dal Prato's first two were written, possibly Panzacchi's first, and the first of the Act I choruses as well. For Mozart the act of composing was not only a matter of putting the notes on paper; there is a certain amount of demonstrable truth behind the old anecdote of his composing in his head, and there is no reason to think he was not doing that during these days as discussion of the opera proceeded. For example, in his letter of 24 November, otherwise largely devoted to gossip (particularly about the famous soprano Madame Mara and her obnoxious husband), his request for a cut in the chorus 'Placido è il mar' suggests that he had some ideas for it running through his mind. (Here he asked if it could break off after the repeat of the chorus following Elettra's first verse, 'or failing that after the second'; as the first printing of the libretto shows, there were originally to have been three solo verses and four appearances of the choral refrain. Leopold readily agreed in his response of 30 November.)

Varesco was quick to prepare the new aria text for Raaff, but it pleased neither Raaff nor Mozart: Mozart complained (29 November) about both its wording and its sense – 'it ought to express peace and contentment . . . we have seen, heard and felt throughout the opera about the trials he has suffered'. Mozart quotes, as a model, four lines from a Metastasio aria from *Achille in Sciro* (curiously, he forgot that he had done so and quoted it again in his next letter, two days later). Then follows one of his most famous remarks:

Tell me, do you not find the speech of the subterranean voice too long? Consider it carefully. – Imagine yourself in the theatre, and that the voice must be terrifying – it must be penetrating – and one must believe that it is real – how can this be believed, when the speech is so long, for during this time the hearer will become increasingly sure that it is meaningless? – If the Ghost's speech in *Hamlet* were not so long it would have a better effect. – This speech can easily be made shorter and will gain more by it than it will lose.

Three days before, Mozart had lunched with Panzacchi. On the following day Raaff came to hear his Act II aria; it is not clear from Mozart's next letter (1 December) whether this was the first time he had heard it – the fact that 'he is as excited by it as a passionate young man with his beloved, for he sings it at night before he goes to sleep and again in the morning when he wakes up' implies that he had been acquainted with it for some days. Mozart wrote of the elderly tenor's contentment with the way the music lay for his voice; he rarely missed an opportunity to impress on his father how successful he had been and how lavish had been the praise heaped on him. The same day, 1 December, saw the first rehearsal with orchestra, at Seeau's house, with a reduced string section, with six violins, but complete wind. 'I cannot tell you how delighted and astonished they all were', Mozart reported; further, the oboist Friedrich Ramm said that no music had ever impressed him so deeply. The next rehearsal was set for a week ahead, when the first act would be done with twelve violins and the second with the small band.

Half-way

Work now proceeded steadily on composition; by this time Mozart seems to have reached about half-way through the second act. In his next letter (5 December) he continued complaining about the words of the Act III aria for Raaff, saying for a third time that he would prefer it to be a one-part aria (that is, a setting of a single quatrain) rather than the more usual form in which the opening words have to return (in one of his comments he says that a second part often gets in his way). One result of the lunch he had been given by Panzacchi – even then there was no such thing as a free lunch – was a request that Arbace's Act III recitative be lengthened: 'we must do what we can to oblige this worthy old fellow', who was a good actor, and the situation invited it. Varesco, it seems, duly obliged. Further, Leopold told Mozart (4 December), he had given Varesco his candid opinion as to the length of the speech for the subterranean voice and expected a shorter version to be forthcoming, and had shown him the Metastasio model for the aria. A week later he sent the new aria for Raaff, with some characteristic advice: 'I advise you when composing to consider not only the musical, but also *the unmusical public*. Remember, for every *ten true connoisseurs* there are a *hundred ignoramuses*. So do not neglect the so-called *popular* style, which tickles *long ears*.' But in the main Leopold's letters about this time deal with matters of local and family interest only, besides preparing and sending Mozart's black suit (the Empress Maria Theresia had just died) and a pair of socks with the conductor of the mail coach.

Mozart responded to Leopold's advice: 'There is music in my opera for all kinds of people, though not for the long-eared.' This letter was written on the day (16 December) of the next rehearsal: Acts I and II with full orchestra, Act III in chamber style – though it was well short of being finished (three days later Mozart still had three arias, a chorus, and the ballet music to write). 'Afterwards, we go straight on to the theatre', he added, presumably for a production rehearsal. The rehearsal was evidently an open one, which at this stage was not unusual; Mozart reported that 'the orchestra and the whole audience discovered that the second act was actually more expressive and original than the first'. But the rehearsal must have shown, too, that further cuts were needed:

The scene between father and son in Act I and the first scene in Act II between Idomeneo and Arbace are both too long. They would certainly bore the audience, particularly as in the first of them both the actors are poor, and in the second one of them is; besides, they are really no more than a narration of what the spectators themselves have already seen. These scenes will be printed as they stand. But I should like the Abbate to indicate how they should be shortened – as drastically as possible – for otherwise I shall have to shorten them myself.

Leopold's response (22 December), which accompanied what had been intended as the definitive text, laid out for the printer, contains the most detailed discussion of the entire correspondence. On receiving Mozart's letter he had summoned Varesco. 'We have considered the first recitative in all its aspects and we see no reason to shorten it', he pompously begins. He points out that originally it was intended that it be even longer, to avoid too speedy a recognition between father and son, and he goes through the scene step by step, explaining its function and how it is designed to establish Idamante's character, to show him as a son 'worthy of his father' (significant words from Leopold) and to arouse 'admiration, respect, and a longing to learn who this youth may be'. Leopold offered Mozart a cut that he reckoned would be harmless, but pooh-poohed the idea of making it:

One and a half pages will thus be omitted – that is, the beautiful description of the heroic deed . . . you would save one *minute*, yes, a whole minute. Great gain, indeed. Or do you want father and son to run up and recognise each other, like a Harlequin and Brighella disguised as servants in a foreign country, meet and instantly embrace?

Mozart did in fact cut, at one stage or another, Idamante's proud description, addressed to this apparent stranger, of his father's heroism at Troy (the full text is printed in the first version of the libretto); as Leopold says, it helps establish the father–son relationship, but it is not essential, and nor, in the event, were other parts of this scene that Mozart omitted. Leopold, however, doubtless because at this stage he saw matters more from Varesco's standpoint than his son's, dug his heels in fairly firmly over cuts. He argued that in a first act no one would be bored anyway, and he repeats that argument for the opening scene of the second. In the long recitative at the beginning of Act II, he would consent only to the abbreviation of a luxuriously long speech of Idomeneo's; besides that, 'not a single word can be omitted without destroying the sense', though he did then suggest one further cut of a few lines. Mozart immediately accepted all these cuts, and went a little beyond them in the recognition scene (probably he had set the entire text at a very early stage, even at Salzburg, and scrapped the sheet these passages were on, substituting another; the use of single folios rather than the usual bifolia at this point hints as much). Red crayon marks in the Munich performing score suggest that at a later stage a few extra bars were omitted over and above these (the Munich source was not available at the time the *NMA* score was prepared and its departures are not shown in it).[4]

When he replied, on 27 December, Mozart was slightly defensive. It had not been his own idea, he said, to shorten these scenes, merely one to which he assented because the actors 'spoil the recitative by singing it with no spirit or fire, and very monotonously. They are the worst actors who ever walked the stage.' He goes on to tell Leopold of the approval his opera had met, from the Elector himself among others; in fact Leopold already knew this, for in a letter that crossed with Mozart's he related the gossip about the opera that had reached Salzburg. There is one particularly interesting observation in Mozart's letter, referring to the difficulties of composing for the vain and inflexible Raaff:

It is hard to compose for him, but easy if you elect to write commonplace arias, as for instance, the first one, 'Vedrommi intorno'. When you hear it, you will say it is good and beautiful – but had I composed it for Zonca it would have been far better suited to the words.

Giovanni Battista Zonca was the Munich bass singer, formerly at Mannheim (there are indications in the autograph that at an early stage Mozart had sketched some of the recitative for a bass, later writing the tenor notes on the same stave; if, as is perfectly possible, Zonca had initially been envisaged as singing Idomeneo, Mozart's remark would have more meaning). Raaff had been complaining about the Act III quartet, which gave him no chance to show off his voice – 'Non c'è da spianar la voce'. 'As if', Mozart responded, 'a quartet should not be more spoken than sung.' 'There is nothing in this opera', he says he told Raaff, 'with which I am more pleased than this quartet.' Raaff complained, too, about the awkward diction in the new text for his last aria, with such a phrase as 'vienmi a rinvigorir' (Mozart had earlier found fault with the verse of the previous version). It is true, Leopold replied (29–30 December), that there are five i's, but he could pronounce the phrase twenty times with rapidity and ease, even if Raaff had found it a tongue-twister. He also made suggestions for the oracle scene:

I imagine you will choose low wind instruments to accompany the subterranean voice. How would it be if, after the *slight* subterranean rumble, the instruments *sustained, or rather began to sustain*, their notes, softly, and then made a *crescendo such as might inspire terror*, and during the *decrescendo the voice would begin to sing*? And there might be a terrifying crescendo at *each phrase uttered by the voice*.

Mozart's next letter again crossed with Leopold's; he was able to tell his father that Raaff was reconciled over the quartet, now that it had been rehearsed (though not without difficulties with Dal Prato, who has 'no method, no intonation, no feeling'), but still 'cannot stomach the "rinvigorir" and "rigiovenir"' at the end of the stanzas of the new final aria. 'To avoid the final shake on the *i* in the first *rinvigorir*, I ought really transfer it to the *o*', Mozart notes.

Raaff had pressed him to substitute tacitly an old and not too well-known Metastasio text, 'Bell'alme al ciel dilette' from *Natal di Giove*, as he felt that Varesco could not be asked for a third version. Another letter followed four days later (3 January 1781): 'My head and my hands are so full of Act III that it would be no wonder if I were to turn into a third act myself', it starts. The subterranean voice, he says, is to be accompanied with just three trombones and two horns, which will be placed with the voice rather than in the orchestra. There are a few more points about Act III, ones that had come up when Mozart got down to detailed work. For example, he lengthened the introduction to the High Priest's recitative 'for safety's sake' so that there was time for Arbace to exit after his aria and then – if necessary – to return. Then he objects to finding the king alone, kneeling, in the temple:

He must come in with his whole retinue. A march must be introduced here, so I have composed a very simple one ... while it is being played, the king appears and the priests prepare the offerings for the sacrifice.

Mozart presents this as if it were simply a matter of getting stage etiquette right, but perhaps more to the point is the fact that he was giving himself the chance to establish the atmosphere of ritual and gravity for this climactic scene. He also refers here to a missing stage direction – 'Partono' ('they depart') – in Elettra's recitative after the utterance of the subterranean voice: 'it seems to me very foolish', he says, 'that they should all rush off so quickly for no reason except to leave Madame Elettra alone'. It would not, in terms of theatrical convention in Mozart's time, normally be acceptable to have the whole company on stage while Elettra sang her aria; but clearly Mozart was unhappy at the notion of clearing the stage simply for that purpose. This was, of course, a flaw in the planning of the libretto.

While he was writing this letter, Mozart received a five-line note from Leopold, enclosing a new aria text – the third, 'Torna la pace' – for Raaff from Varesco. The note (sent on 1 January) is lost, but on 4 January Leopold wrote again telling Mozart of a contretemps with Varesco about the new aria; the chaplain had apparently been enraged and complained about his fee, but ended up by saying that he would go away and see whether anything occurred to him. Evidently something did, but he still preferred the previous text for the aria, 'Sazio è il destin', in spite of its awkward diction, and demanded that it be printed in the libretto even if a different aria were set and sung. This may serve as a salutary reminder that during most of the eighteenth century the librettist, often of superior social station to the musician, was generally considered creatively the more important of the two; it was only with Mozart's time that this began to change.

In his next letter (10–11 January) Mozart could report that all he had to write was some ballet music; also that the première had been postponed until 29 January, which 'will give us opportunity for further and more careful rehearsals'. He mentions, too, that he had a 'desperate fight' with Seeau over the trombones: 'I had to be rude to him as otherwise I should never have got my way.' As we shall see, he probably did not get his way in the end. Mozart's last letter followed on 18 January, reporting briefly on the rehearsal of Act IV, which 'went off splendidly; it was considered much superior to the first two acts'. But, he continues, the libretto is too long, and so accordingly is the music. The plan was now to omit two arias, Idamante's 'No, la morte io non pavento': 'in any case, it is out of place there' – a reasonable comment, as it does indeed delay the action at a critical point, just before the intended sacrifice – and, he announces surprisingly coolly, Raaff's last aria. This was the one for which Varesco had written the text three times over; but 'we must make a virtue of necessity'. This must have been difficult for him to accept, for the last scene is in danger of seeming perfunctory without it. There was still Elettra's aria, but it had always been intended that there be a lyrical number after her storming off, originally a quartet for the lovers, Idomeneo and Arbace, then the aria for Raaff. Mozart, as we have seen, had hoped for a short, single-stanza aria here, but Varesco supplied a full-length text and the one Mozart set and promptly had to abandon was an expansive piece, no doubt partly to flatter Raaff but also surely because he felt that something of the kind was appropriate. 'Torna la pace' is in three sections, a B♭ *adagio* ending in F, a $\frac{3}{8}$ *allegretto*, and a recapitulation of the *adagio*, now adjusted to end in the home key. When it is performed today, very often only the third part is sung.

Run-up to performance

At this point the Mozart family correspondence comes to an end as an informative source about the genesis of the opera and its première; Leopold and Nannerl Mozart left for Munich on 25 January. Further changes, however, do seem to have been made in the work, and to some extent these can be inferred from the libretto and the surviving performance material.

Two versions of the libretto were printed. The earlier was presumably set in type some time after 22 December, when Mozart received the 'definitive text'; it embodies none of the cuts, even those agreed much earlier, and clearly the intention was still to use Varesco's complete text, not excluding items that would be omitted, as the poet required and the Mozarts (and, after some argument, Seeau) had accepted. This is a bilingual libretto, of the usual kind, with the Italian on the versos and the German translation, by Johann Andreas Schachtner, on the rectos. The second libretto is in Italian only; some of it seems to use the same typesetting but other sections, even where unaltered, are reset. It accommodates the changes made just beyond the time, it would seem, of Mozart's last letter, and it served as the basis for the main musical text in the *Neue Mozart Ausgabe* (1973). Clearly it was produced when it came to be realised that the opera had been altered too much for the original text to be appropriate for use during the performance. In the first two acts the changes, six in all, are largely confined to recitative: two each in the recognition scene and in the first scene of Act II, a couple of lines at the start of Scene 6 and the abbreviating of 'Placido è il mar'.

The Act III cuts shown in the libretto are much more extensive. The arias for Idamante and Idomeneo are missing, as the correspondence would lead us to expect. What is more, it indicates that another aria was cut in Act III, Elettra's 'D'Oreste, d'Aiace', in place of which there is a shorter version of the accompanied recitative that had preceded it, adjusted to provide a fiery exit.[5] The assembled company, then, did not after all have to move off to allow Elettra her aria; instead, she sang her short piece, and 'parte infuriata', leaving everyone else to rejoicing. Cuts just before and in the temple scene are also shown: there are reduced texts for both 'Oh voto tremendo!' and 'Accogli, oh re del mar', the former shorn of the opening *A–B* of its *A–B–A* structure, the latter foreshortened to remove Idomeneo's solo and the brief rounding-off by the priests (both these cuts are indicated by 'Vi-de' marks in the *NMA* score). The first libretto shows a much longer text for the final chorus, 'Scenda Amor'; Mozart never set it, doubtless having realised by the time he reached that point that cutting would be needed. The librettos differ, too, in the text for the Oracle (to which we shall return).

It is, however, far from certain that the second libretto does in fact represent exactly what was performed. Since the preparation of the *NMA* score, further material has become available. Of the autograph score, only Act III could be used by the *NMA* editor, Daniel Heartz; since then the bulk of the Mozart material formerly in Berlin has come to light in the Biblioteka Jagiellońska, Kraków, including the autograph scores of Acts I and II. These do not, in fact, very much affect the situation, since they had served as the basis for the old complete edition of 1881 and for the other secondary manuscript used by Heartz. More crucial is the discovery (by Robert Münster)[6] in the Bayerische Staatsoper archives of the remainder of the transcript of the work by a court copyist, of which only Act III had previously been known; this was the performing score in 1781.

Many of the changes indicated in this new source are in the recitative. But others, marked in ink or in red crayon – implying two layers of changes, made at different times, the latter type the later – affect the lyrical music. In Act I, the cadenzas in Idamante's aria are cut out; this seems understandable in the light of Mozart's remarks about Dal Prato. In the so-called 'intermezzo', the choral scene 'Nettuno s'onori', there is a substantial cut, covering bars 81–159 – removing what is essentially one appearance of the rondo refrain and one episode, the G major one for two sopranos ('Su conca d'oro'). In Act II, cadenzas are dropped in the arias for Arbace and Idomeneo ('Fuor del mar'), and Elettra's aria 'Idol mio' is shortened slightly, by the omission of two eight-bar phrases. Further, the preceding secco recitative for Elettra and Idomeneo, which stood in the original between 'Fuor del mar' and her accompanied recitative (which surely succeeds his big aria too speedily in the standard version) is restored, an additional seventeen bars. None of these changes is indicated in the later libretto.

In Act III the Munich source shows changes that are more radical. These were not incorporated in the *NMA* text. The duet for Ilia and Idamante, 'S'io non moro', is wholly struck out, and a new cadence is provided to link the first scene and the third. Then the scene for Arbace is wholly deleted, both the great accompanied recitative ('Sventurata Sidon!') in which he mourns the state of his country and his ensuing aria, 'Se colà ne'fati è scritto'. (There are, Münster points out, already indications of both these cuts in the autograph, also in red crayon.) In the temple scene, the music for the High Priest is transposed down an octave in the Munich score, which is surprising if indeed the part was sung, as is generally supposed, by the tenor Giovanni Valesi; if in fact the role were to have been taken over by a bass, much of it would lie in a register that could well be ineffective with the orchestral music scored as it is. But still more surprisingly, Idamante's aria 'Nò, la morte' – the one that Mozart thought 'out of place', and which is clearly struck out in the autograph and excluded from the second printing of the libretto – is shown as included, with an unambiguous 'segue aria' indication. Could it have been restored, at the last moment, for the performances? Perhaps Dal Prato had influential friends at court who pressed Seeau and Mozart to let him have his aria rather than merely a duet. There are other changes in the closing scenes. The arias for Elettra and Idomeneo are still excluded; so too is the deeply poetic E♭ prefatory music to Idomeneo's final recitative (which is also struck out in the autograph), and the closing chorus, as in the autograph, consists of only its basic seventy-five bars: that is, without the central instrumental section or the da capo.

In his letter of 10–11 January Mozart had referred to his 'desperate fight' with Seeau over the three trombones for the oracle scene; these, not being a part of the normal orchestra, would need to have been specially engaged at extra expense. Four versions survive of this number, as shown in Table 2.1. No. 28c is a setting of what is probably the complete Varesco text, as printed in the first libretto (unless the original was longer still), which he already thought was 'far too long' before he even set it; he is unlikely to have done so before his letter of 29 November, when it is first mentioned. The texts for the other versions are all extracted, in different ways, from this, one of them presumably being the shortened version by Varesco that Leopold reported having requested from him on 4 December. 28a, c and d all appear in the autograph score, but 28c and d are deleted, leaving the perfunctorily brief 28a seemingly having won the day. This is the only setting that does not use Leopold's proposed crescendos to herald the oracle's words. But would Seeau, if doubtful about the cost of trombones for a couple of minutes' music, have consented to their hire for a puny eight bars' music and one bar's rest? Whatever the case, it was 28b, without trombones, that was favoured at the time the second libretto went to print, and its presence in the Munich performing score appears to bear this out.[7] So unless there was another change of heart it seems that Mozart's 'rudeness' failed and he did not after all get his way over the trombones. It seems, too, that

Table 2.1

NMA No./p.	Bars	Instruments	Text beginning
28a/472	9	2 horns, 3 trombones	Idomeneo cessi esser re
28b/472	44	2 clarinets, 2 bassoons, 2 horns	A Idomeneo perdona
28c/566	70	2 horns, 3 trombones	Ha vinto Amore . . . a Idomeneo perdona
28d/568	31	2 horns, 3 trombones	Ha vinto Amore . . . Idomeneo cessi esser re

although as late as 18 January he still thought the speech 'far too long', and he said he was shortening it again (this may be when he composed 28a), he decided finally in favour of an utterance of moderate length.

It seems clear, then, that between his last letter to Leopold (18 January) and the première Mozart was compelled to make still further adjustments, mostly but not exclusively cuts. The reasons for the restoration of a few passages of recitative previously cut we can only guess at: probably in the event the short versions worked poorly on the stage or created difficulties in the dramatic timing. The cuts were presumably needed simply because the opera was so long; it seems clear, in retrospect, as indeed Mozart said, that the libretto was too extended, at least for the kind of treatment – Mozart's arias, here as elsewhere, are nearly always longer than those of his contemporaries – he had in mind. It is not, of course, possible to be sure exactly at what stage some of the cuts were made. *Idomeneo* may have had as few as three performances. These were on 29 January and on 5 and 12 February; further performances were planned for 19 or 26 February, but on 19 February there was a court banquet in honour of the Duke of Zweibrücken and on 26 February a fancy-dress ball, and the evidence seems to indicate that the opera performances, or at least the one proposed for 19 February, were cancelled. The performance on 12 February was in fact followed by a ball, some ten minutes away from the opera house, starting at 9.30 p.m.; the opera had begun at 5.30 p.m. The possibility of the cuts having been instituted only for nights when the performance had to finish early cannot be ruled out, but that would not account either for the restored passages, which are indicated in the same way, or for the parallel red crayon markings

Table 2.2

Act III		1	2	3
R. 19	Solitudini amiche	x	m	x
19	Zeffiretti, lusinghieri	x	m	x
R. 20	Ei stesso vien	x	m	x
	Principessa, a' tuoi	x	m	s
20 a	S'io non moro	x	m	
20 b	Spiegarti non poss'io			
	(substituted for Vienna, 1786)			
R. 21	(Cieli? che vedo?)	x	m	x
21	Andrò, ramingo e solo	x	m	x
	(modified for Vienna, 1786)			
R. 22	Sire, alla reggia	x	m	x
22	Sventurata Sidon!	x	m	
22	Se colà ne' fati	x	m	
23	Volgi intorno	x	m	x
24	Oh voto tremendo!	x	m	s
25	March	x	m	x
26	Accogli, oh re del mar	x	m	s
	Stupenda vittoria!	x	m	x
	Qual risuona . . . Sire	x	m	x
27	Padre, mio caro padre	x	m	x
27 a	Nò, la morte	x	a	x
	Ma che più tardi?	x	m	x
	Ferma, o sire	x	s	s
28 a	Idomeneo cesser esse re	x	m	
28 b	A Idomeneo perdona		m	x
28 c	Ha vinto Amore	x	a	
28 d	Ha vinto Amore	x	a	
29	Oh ciel pietoso!			
	[59 bars]	x	a	
	Oh ciel pietoso!			
	[30 bars]		m	x
	D'Oreste, d'Aiace	x	a	
30	Popoli, a voi	x	m	s
30 a	Torna la pace	x	a	
31	Scenda Amor	x	m	s

Key:
x = included, s = shortened
Column 1: as originally composed
Column 2: *NMA* (m = main text, a = in appendix)
Column 3: Munich performance score

in the autograph (which Mozart would by then have reclaimed and which would not normally have been used as a working copy).

After Munich

When Mozart left Munich, in March 1781, it was not to return to Salzburg; he had been summoned to attend the Archbishop in Vienna, and within two months there ensued the famous and terminal quarrel with the Salzburg authorities which resulted in Mozart's spending the remainder of his life as a freelance composer in Vienna. *Idomeneo* was very much in Mozart's mind. He wanted, soon after arriving in Vienna, to play it through to the emperor (letter of 24 March), and though that was not managed he did in May 1781 play it to Count Orsini-Rosenberg, the court theatre director, and other prominent people (Sonnenfels and van Swieten) at the house of Countess Thun, who retained the score for several weeks (letters of 26 May and 27 June). On 12 September he told his father that he had hoped that there would be a chance of a Viennese production during a visit by Russian royalty, but to his irritation two Gluck operas were to be given. He writes:

The translator of *Iphigénie [en Tauride]* into German is an excellent poet and I would have been happy to have him translate my Munich opera. I would have altered Idomeneo's role completely and made it a bass part for Fischer. I would have made several other changes and arranged it more in the French style. Mme Bernasconi, Adamberger and Fischer would have been delighted to sing it, but as they now have two operas to learn, and such exhausting ones, I have to excuse them.

Clearly Mozart had in mind a bass Idomeneo (as a king would normally be in a French opera; Ludwig Fischer was later to sing Osmin in *Die Entführung*) and a tenor Idamante (Valentin Adamberger was to sing Belmonte). The following January, Mozart reports, his friends, including Adamberger, were advising him to perform scenes from the opera during a concert at the theatre (letter of 23 January); he may have done so in a concert on 3 March, and certainly did on 23 March 1783, when he included 'Se il padre perdei' in a Lenten season programme (letter of 29 March). He had hopes of giving the entire opera in a concert in 1784, but never did so. An anecdote about a family performance of the Act III quartet during his and Constanze's visit to Salzburg in the summer of 1783, at which Mozart was so overcome with emotion that he wept and had to leave the room, is related by Mary Novello.[9]

An opportunity to perform the work did, however, arise in 1786, at the time when Mozart was composing *Le nozze di Figaro*. Little is known about the circumstances. The work was given on 13 March in the theatre attached to the Auersperg Palace, almost certainly in concert form – acted and costumed stage performances were forbidden during Lent, and in any case the cast was amateur. Idomeneo was sung by Giuseppe Antonio Bridi, Idamante by Baron Pulini, Ilia by Anna von Pufendorf and Elettra by Countess Hatzfeld. The part of Arbace was omitted. A notice of the performance, in the Salzburg periodical *Pfeffer und Salz*, indicates that Mozart's work 'did not receive the degree of approbation that is generally accorded to his art when he plays on the fortepiano'.[10]

The two versions

Discussion of *Idomeneo* and its text often involves references to 'the Munich version' (with Idamante sung by a soprano or mezzo) and 'the Vienna version' (with Idamante a tenor). These terms are not quite as clear-cut as they might appear. As we have seen, a good deal of doubt surrounds what 'the Munich version' actually is; and the Vienna version, too, is hedged about with uncertainties. That Idamante was sung by a tenor is usually taken for granted, and certainly it is unlikely that Baron Pulini was a castrato. But there exists no clear, authoritative text in which the part of Idamante as a whole is shown as a tenor one. Mozart made four major changes for the Vienna performances: he composed a new aria, in the fashionable rondò form (that is, slow–fast, using a gavotte-type rhythm), for Idamante, K. 490, to replace the Arbace aria at the opening of Act II; he provided a new and more succinct duet for Ilia and Idamante, K. 489, in place of the existing one (thirty-nine bars in a single tempo rather than a two-movement 107 bars); he adjusted the two ensembles including Idamante (the terzet at the end of Act II and the quartet in Act III) for the different singer; and he prepared a simplified version of the very demanding aria for Idomeneo in Act II, 'Fuor del mar'. Idamante's arias in the first and third acts, if they were given, were presumably transposed down an octave.

This would all be perfectly straightforward had Mozart simply composed, or recomposed, these pieces with a tenor. The rondò, however, to the words 'Non temer, amato bene', is actually notated in the soprano clef, an octave above the pitch at which a tenor would sing it. Mozart did not normally make mistakes of that kind; sound and symbol were one to him, and if he wrote in the soprano clef we may be reasonably sure that he was imagining a soprano voice, male or female. The aria, an extended one prefaced by an accompanied recitative, and with a violin obbligato (intended for his violinist friend Count Hatzfeld), is in fact written in such a way that a soprano voice would be much more effective than a tenor. No answer to this enigma suggests itself. The mystery is compounded by the notation of the other new item, the duet: here Mozart wrote two soprano clefs for the singers, then proceeded to notate the music for Idamante as if the clef were a tenor. This can only be a 'clerical' slip. Then, in the quartet, Idamante's new part is again notated in the soprano clef, but the writing is implausibly high and the music must have been intended to be sung an octave lower. One may devise explanations – that the habit of writing a soprano clef for Idamante was too deeply set to be discarded, at least without conscious effort, or that the original intention for this performance had been to use a castrato or indeed a woman.[11] In the terzet and the quartet all the voice parts were written out afresh. Idamante's is essentially as before, at the same sounding pitch where the music previously lay low, an octave lower where it did not; in the quartet the music for Ilia and Elettra is at some points exchanged, presumably to suit the capacities of the singers (much in the manner that Mozart later juggled the parts for the Countess and Susanna in the various versions of *Figaro*). Speculation about these anomalies would be more fruitful if we had a clearer idea about the intentions for this performance or the order in which Mozart composed and adapted the various numbers.

All the new Viennese material is written on the same paper-type, one that Mozart used in other works of 1785–6. The two new numbers are wholly written on this paper, and are dated 10 March 1786. This paper was used for the revised vocal parts for the quartet (the revisions for the terzet are missing from the auto-graph) and for a few odd sheets where the recitative needed to be adjusted to accommodate the alterations. The changes in 'Fuor del mar' are also written on this paper. Scholars have long thought it likely that the simplified, shortened version of this aria was prepared in Munich because the original was too demanding for Raaff (as indeed Mozart said in his letter of 15 November), but the simpler version does not appear in the Munich performing score and the paper evidence puts it beyond doubt that it was Bridi, not Raaff, who balked at its demands, or whom Mozart could not trust to meet them.

There is no reference to *Idomeneo* in any known Mozart letter or other document after 1786. Unless he performed music from it at one of his concerts, he never heard a note of his grand opera, his *operone*, again.[12]

3 'Madame Dorothea Wendling is arcicontentissima': the performers of Idomeneo

MARK EVERIST

When Mozart received the commission for *Idomeneo* and began work on the opera, he knew that he would be writing for some of the best singers in Europe and for one of its finest orchestras.[1] The principal tenor was to be Anton Raaff (Idomeneo), then aged sixty-six and at the end of a career that had started with study under Bernacchi in the late 1730s. He had worked with Jommelli in Vienna, dominated tenor roles in Italy in the 1760s, and concluded his career in the service of Karl Theodor in Mannheim and Munich.[2] While he was at Mannheim in the 1770s, Raaff shared the stage with Dorothea Wendling (Ilia), who was considered by the aesthetician Christian Schubart and Wilhelm Heinse, the novelist, to be one of Europe's finest sopranos.[3] Christoph Wieland thought her superior even to the famous Gertrud Elisabeth Mara.[4] The wife of Dorothea Wendling's brother-in-law, Elisabeth Wendling (Elettra), had been praised by Leopold Mozart in 1763.[5] Since four participants in the première of *Idomeneo* were named Wendling, a fragment of their family tree is given as Figure 3.1.[6]

The orchestra was effectively the same that had so impressed Charles Burney among others. In August 1772 he described it in words that have since become famous: 'There are more solo

Figure 3.1

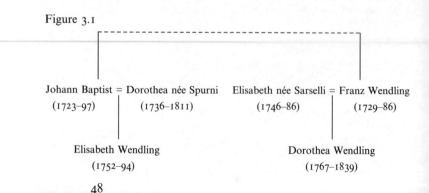

Johann Baptist = Dorothea née Spurni   Elisabeth née Sarselli = Franz Wendling
(1723–97)   (1736–1811)   (1746–86)   (1729–86)

Elisabeth Wendling   Dorothea Wendling
(1752–94)   (1767–1839)

48

players, and good composers in this, than perhaps in any other orchestra in Europe; it is an army of generals, equally fit to plan a battle, as to fight it.'[7]

More important to Mozart than the international fame of at least two of his principals was the fact that he was familiar with the musical capabilities of most of the singers and many of the instrumentalists; many of them had been his personal friends from at least the end of 1777, and some for much longer. Mozart's attitude towards writing for singers and instrumentalists coloured the way he composed. It is possible to show, both from documentary accounts of the composition of *Idomeneo* and from an examination of Mozart's earlier encounters with the same performers, how the strengths and prejudices of the artists played a role in shaping the work.

Table 3.1 gives the cast-lists both for the Munich performances of *Idomeneo* and for the 1786 Vienna revival (see chapter 2, above). It also includes the singers' ages at the time of the performances and their dates.

Table 3.1. Cast-lists for *Idomeneo*

	Munich, 1781	Vienna, 1786
Idomeneo	Anton Raaff (sixty-six) (1714–97)	Giuseppe Antonio Bridi (twenty-two) (1763–1836)
Idamante	Vincenzo dal Prato (twenty-four) (1756–1826)	Baron Pulini
Ilia	Dorothea Wendling (forty-four) (1736–1811)	Anna von Pufendorf (twenty-eight) (1757–1843)
Elettra	Elisabeth Wendling (thirty-four) (1746–86)	Maria Anna Hortensia, Gräfin Hatzfeld
Arbace	Domenico de Panzacchi (forty-seven) (1733–1805)	
High Priest	Giovanni Valesi (forty-five) (1735–1816)	

The cast was a highly varied group. Beside the 'stars' already mentioned, there was the castrato Vincenzo dal Prato (Idamante) who was relatively inexperienced, and little is known about Domenico de Panzacchi (Arbace). Giovanni Valesi (High Priest) was recognised more as a teacher, his pupils including Johann Valentin Adamberger, the first Belmonte in *Die Entführung aus dem Serail*, and Carl Maria von Weber.[8] Panzacchi, Valesi, dal Prato, and Elisabeth Wendling were not very familiar to Mozart, although he had heard the latter as Anna in Holzbauer's *Günther von Schwarzburg* in November 1777 at Mannheim.[9] Valesi may have sung in the première of Mozart's *La finta giardiniera* in Munich on 13 January 1775.[10] Dorothea Wendling and Raaff were old friends of Mozart. As long ago as 19 August 1763, Leopold Mozart had written to his landlord, Lorenz Hagenhauer, from the summer residence of the Elector of Mannheim to praise the orchestra, and singled out Dorothea's husband Johann Baptist Wendling as a strikingly talented flautist. A week after his arrival in Mannheim in 1777, Mozart was taken to meet Wendling (letter of 8 November), and, despite the difference of thirty years in their ages, they developed a very close relationship. Wendling was in Paris at the same time as Mozart in the spring of 1778, and they remained in contact at least until October 1790, when they met in Frankfurt-am-Main. Mozart was close to the whole family, and wrote music not just for Johann Baptist and Dorothea but also for their daughter Elisabeth who, as Mozart told his father (twice) had been the Elector's mistress.[11]

The other senior figure in the Mannheim–Munich orchestra in whose company Mozart spent much time was Christian Cannabich, the leader of the orchestra, whom the family had known since 1766.[12] Cannabich was the first person to whom Mozart was taken when he arrived in Mannheim (letter of 31 October 1777), and five days later (4 November) he reported to his father that he was with Cannabich every day. Mozart wrote no music for him; of all the colleagues he encountered in Mannheim and Munich, Cannabich was the composer to whom he was closest, and this may well account for the fact that Mozart was reluctant to write for him, for as leader of the orchestra, his virtuosity lay as much in direction as, in the case of Wendling, for example, in execution.[13]

Anton Raaff

Raaff was another close friend; on the day that Mozart first met Cannabich in Mannheim, he also met the famous tenor, and Raaff was to remain close to Mozart and his family for several years.[14]

Unlike the unstinting praise offered to most of the Mannheim–
Munich singers and instrumentalists, the respect Mozart had for
Raaff was qualified by serious musical reservations. Raaff had taken
the tenor role in the same performance of *Günther von Schwarzburg*
in which Mozart had heard Elisabeth Wendling in 1777; both
Mozart and his mother wrote to Leopold about him. Maria Anna
Mozart generously observed that he must have been a good singer
in his time but that his voice was beginning to fail; she compared
him unfavourably with the Salzburg bass, Joseph Meissner. Mozart
was not only unimpressed with Raaff's performance but was prepared to joke about it with Wendling (letters of 14 November 1777).

But Mozart was a good critic. The letter he wrote to his father
in Paris on 12 June the following year is partly about French tastes
and the way in which he had carefully composed the symphony
K. 297. Most of it, however, consists of a reasoned alteration of his
views on Raaff, and as a major composer's considered opinion of
an important singer it is a significant document. Mozart first of all
relates his previous objections to Raaff, and begins to give the singer
the benefit of the doubt: he had only heard Raaff in a rehearsal of
the Holzbauer opera 'with his hat on and a stick in his hand', and
he admits that many of Raaff's characteristics may stem from the
fact that he trained with Bernacchi whose school was not, as
Mozart also admits, to his taste. His comments are based on a
performance Raaff gave at the 'Concert spirituel' on 28 May of J. C.
Bach's aria 'Non so d'onde viene', a text that Mozart was to set
for Aloysia Weber later that year and for Ludwig Fischer in 1787
(K. 294 and 512.)[15]

Mozart's letter continues with a more detailed comparison
between Raaff and Meissner, although – as he had not heard either
in their prime – he makes it clear that he is talking in general terms
rather than about their specific effect. On the whole, he prefers
Raaff to Meissner except in cantabile, and he notes that Raaff
indulges too much in this style – even though it must have been
effective in his youth.[16] He points to a variety of strengths in Raaff's
execution: bravura singing, diction, chest voice, and his manner of
singing short andantino movements. In the light of the well-
documented statements by Mozart that he regarded the duty of a
composer as making the music fit the singer like a suit of clothes,
it is therefore not surprising that it is possible to follow through
all these observations into acts of compositional choice eighteen
months later when Mozart came to write Raaff's arias for *Idomeneo*.

Example 3.1

a No. 30a

b K.295

One of these, 'Torna la pace' (No. 30a), has striking similarities with the concert aria 'Se al labbro mio non credi' (K. 295), composed for Raaff three years earlier in Mannheim.[17] Both exploit the cantabile that Raaff loved so much, and both employ what by *c.*1780 was an archaic structure: a ternary plan with a central $\frac{3}{8}$ allegretto. This is surely the type of andantino movement to which Mozart was referring in his letter from Paris. Daniel Heartz has clearly shown how the model for both these arias is Metastasio's favourite composer, J. A. Hasse (1699–1783), and how the opening theme from 'Torna la pace' is derived from a cadential formula in 'Se al labbro mio non credi'.[18] Ex. 3.1 compares the opening of the two arias (note the same tempo marking and key).

The various stages in writing Raaff's Act III aria posed substantial problems both for Mozart and especially for Varesco, who

was repeatedly asked for a suitable poem. At one point in the trans-
actions, Mozart and (indirectly) Raaff concentrate at length on the
problems of the last two words of the first line of one of Varesco's
poems, 'Il cor languiva ed era', in terms that make Mozart's
claims about Raaff's diction ring true. Even Leopold was prepared
to concede that Varesco's lines were severely problematic.[19]

Raaff had already asked Mozart to shorten the first version of
'Se al labbro mio non credi' (letter of 28 February 1778). Both
versions survive, and it is clear that Mozart fulfilled Raaff's
wishes. The Act II aria for Idomeneo, 'Fuor del mar', is a bravura
aria designed to exploit another of Raaff's strengths that Mozart
identified in the letter of 12 June 1778. The longer version (12a) is
replete with elaborate coloratura that is intensified in the reprise
(the shorter version (12b), which eliminates all the bravura material,
was written for the Vienna performance of 1786: see chapter 2, p. 46
above). Nevertheless, it is clear from Mozart's work with Raaff
that the composer handled the singer's range with great care. Quite
why Raaff asked Mozart to shorten 'Se al labbro' is uncertain; the
elaborate coloratura in 'Fuor del mar' was either not a problem
or one that Raaff (and implicitly Mozart) could not acknowledge.
Questions of range, however, were different. Figure 3.2 gives the
ranges of Raaff's arias from *Idomeneo* compared with the aria
Mozart heard him sing at the 'Concert spirituel' and the one he
had already written for him.

Figure 3.2

J. C. Bach, 'Non so d'onde viene' (1762):

'Se al labbro' K. 295 (1778):

'Vedrommi intorno' (No. 6, 1781):

'Fuor del mar' (Nos. 12a and b, 1781–6):

'Torna la pace' (No. 30a, 1781):

Worth noting is the contracting range in the *Idomeneo* arias. The pitch a' is only found once in Raaff's solo arias, and that is as an appoggiatura in 'Torna la pace' (No. 30a, bar 35); the exposed and repeated b♭ of 'Se al labbro' is completely absent.

Of all the materials surviving from *Idomeneo*, one of the most interesting documents that betray Mozart's working methods is the vocal draft for 'Torna la pace'.[20] It consists of the aria for voice and bass except in orchestral passages where violin 1 and bass are given. Clearly not a composition sketch, it is probably a draft for Raaff's approval and from which he could learn the aria. It seems highly likely that, as Heartz proposes, the arias to Act I were drafted in this form before Mozart left Salzburg.[21] Only a week after Mozart reached Munich (letter of 8 November), he claimed that Dorothea Wendling was 'arcicontentissima' with her Act I *scena* (R. 1, No. 1). A week later Mozart was able to report that both Wendlings were well pleased with their arias, and Raaff was happy with 'Vedrommi intorno' (letter of 15 November).

Dorothea Wendling

Mozart could only work in advance with any conviction because he knew the singers so well and had written for most of them before. Raaff, although problematic, was a known quantity, and Mozart had already written 'Basta, vincesti' – 'Ah, non lasciarmi, no' K. 295a for Dorothea Wendling; this dates from the same time as 'Se al labbro', February 1778.[22] And exactly in the same way that he modelled Raaff's Act III aria on the 1778 concert aria, so he modelled Dorothea Wendling's *scena* on 'Basta, vincesti'. Both arias are cast in flat-side keys, and a comparison of ranges between 'Ah non lasciarmi' and Ilia's *Idomeneo* arias shows no detectable difference. The 1778 recitative is substantially less elaborate than the one from *Idomeneo*, but even in the earlier passage, changes of tempo are mixed with harmonic twists such as the fifth and sixth bars, as can be seen in Ex. 3.2. This example also compares the very similar openings of the two recitatives; note especially the identical tempo indications. While Mozart would hardly have been insensitive to the correspondence between the characters of Dido and Ilia, it was certainly the extraordinarily elaborate recitative that earned Dorothea Wendling's approval. With its mixture of accompanied and simple recitative and its rapid shifts of tempo and mood, it represents a massive scaling-up of the 1778 model to six times its length. When

Example 3.2

gra - to.

Mozart came to negotiate the shift from recitative to aria, he chose similar techniques: a short three- or four-bar introduction leading straight into a presentation of the soloist with the first theme. An opening on the dominant of the mediant (V of G minor within the domain of E♭), and shifts to V$^0_5$ of the tonic with a change of dynamic, are clearly mirrored in the deceptive cadence and diminished seventh of the *Idomeneo* introduction. The two passages are compared in Ex. 3.3.

The woodwind quartet

From the context of Mozart's comments to his father on 8 November 1780, it is clear that although most of the first act was already composed in one form or another, one of the most interesting numbers from the point of view of the performers was still in gestation. While asking Varesco to rewrite the text of Ilia's Act II aria to eliminate the aside (see chapter 2, p. 28, above), he adds that 'we have agreed to introduce here an aria andantino with obbligatos for four wind-instruments, that is flute, oboe, horn, and bassoon'. The aria was, of course, again written for Dorothea Wendling, and we can be certain of the players' names of three of the four solo instruments: Johann Baptist Wendling (flute), Friedrich Ramm (oboe), and Georg Wenzel Ritter (bassoon). The horn player could have been any one of Georg Eck, or the two Lang brothers, Franz Joseph or Martin Alexander.[23]

This was not a new team. Not only had they been playing together in Munich since 1778, but Wendling and Ramm had been stars of the Mannheim orchestra. Ramm was the inspiration behind Mozart's Oboe Quartet K. 370, and had been an enthusiastic proponent of the Oboe Concerto K. 314, which he had performed five times between early November 1777 and February 1778. Mozart

Example 3.3

may also have started a concerto in F for him (K. 416f), of which only a fragment remains. Much more significantly, Mozart had encountered all three players in Paris in the spring of 1778.

Jean-Joseph Cambini and the *Symphonie concertante* were all the rage when Mozart was in Paris. Mozart announced his determination to contribute to the genre in a letter to his father (5 April 1778), and not only named the three players he would meet again in Munich, Wendling, Cannabich, and Ritter, but claimed that probably the finest player in Europe, the travelling virtuoso Giovanni Punto, would take the horn part. The subsequent intrigue resulted in the four players indeed performing together, but in a work by Cambini.[24] The confusions and contradictions in Mozart's correspondence with Leopold (1 May 1778) may hide nothing more than a straightforward struggle that Mozart lost. The important links between the *symphonie concertante* that Mozart wrote for these players and 'Se il padre perdei' are stressed by Robert Levin, who believes that the work survives in part as the Sinfonia concertante in E♭ K. 297b: an important part of Levin's evidence is a comparison between the woodwind writing in K. 297b and 'Se il padre perdei'.[25]

Vincenzo dal Prato

In Mozart's letter to his father from Paris where he revises his view of Raaff's singing, he admits that he had not seen him act either in *Günther von Schwarzburg* or, of course, at the 'Concert spirituel'. Subsequent events might have made him wish that he had. His first impression of Raaff in Munich was his inability to act: 'Raaff is like a statue' (8 November 1780). His response to this problem was simply an exercise in damage limitation. On 19 December 1780, he wrote to his father asking Varesco to shorten both the dialogue in which Raaff figured with dal Prato in Act I and with Panzacchi in Act II: 'They would certainly bore the audience, particularly as in the first scene both the actors are bad, and in the second, one of them is.' Mozart adopted exactly the opposite procedure when he felt that the acting skills of the singer were being underused; a fortnight earlier, he had requested that Arbace's recitative in Act III should be extended, mostly because the effect that Panzacchi was likely to make on the stage would be favourable.

The scene in Act I between Idomeneo and Idamante described by Mozart in the same letter was played by the oldest and youngest actors on the stage. The picture Mozart painted of dal Prato could not have been bleaker: he was no better actor than Raaff, and he was a lamentable singer.[26] Although Mozart did indeed cut the Idomeneo–Idamante recitative in the first act, much of what appears in the correspondence between Mozart and his father may have been motivated by other considerations. In the letter of 8 November, his first from Munich, Mozart claims that dal Prato's breath gives out in the middle of the aria, and he further alleges that he has no stage experience. But these comments are prefaced by an admission that Mozart had not met dal Prato, and that he is depending on reports from third parties. On the strength of those reports, he suggests that dal Prato is worse than Francesco Ceccarelli, the Salzburg castrato, who was a close friend of the Mozarts.[27] When Mozart writes to his father on 13 November 1780, he lists the names of all those who congratulate Leopold on his name day; he includes dal Prato at the end – but only because he happens to be in the room. Judging from Mozart's subsequent comments, the only reason that he was likely to be in a room with Mozart was because the latter was functioning as his repetiteur: Mozart reported on 15 November that he would have to teach the castrato the whole opera, and a week later (22 November) complains that he has to teach him his whole part 'as if he were a child. He has not a farthing's worth of method.' Mozart's report on dal Prato's performance in a concert on 21 November is blunt: he sang disgracefully and is rotten to the core.

On the strength of Mozart's comments, dal Prato is occasionally described as a novice. But he had made his debut in Fano in 1772 at the age of 16 and had sung at Stuttgart for the future Tsar Paul I a year before Mozart met him.[28] Dal Prato had shared the stage with Valesi at the Teatro San Benedetto in Venice in 1773; the two singers participated in a production of Giacomo Insanguine's *La Merope*.[29] Furthermore, Raaff himself, in a letter to Padre Martini less than a year later, described dal Prato as 'a learned youth, diligent, with the most honest character and the best morals'.[30] This evidence certainly conflicts with Mozart's comments. There is a possibility that, however bad dal Prato may have been (and he may well not have been in the same league as the rest of the cast), Mozart's view of him may have been coloured by his anxiety to promote his friend Ceccarelli; in the letter of 15 November, he even suggests that Ceccarelli might take over dal Prato's position when the latter's contract expired at the end of the year.

Vienna 1781–2

Mozart's first year in Vienna was crowned with the success of *Die Entführung aus dem Serail* on 7 July 1782, and he had been occupied with this work since the very end of July 1781. However, it was not until the première of *Die Entführung* that he finally gave up the hopes that he had been nurturing since his arrival of putting on a production of *Idomeneo* in Vienna. His thoughts about such a course of action were largely determined by the singers available at the Burgtheater. As early as 24 March 1781, Mozart had written to his father about his desire to discuss with the emperor plans to mount a production in Vienna, and by 12 September he was in a position to tell Leopold that Antonia Bernasconi, Ludwig Fischer, and Josef-Valentin Adamberger would be happy to sing in it. Mozart's hopes of putting on a production of *Idomeneo* in German were raised by the translation of Gluck's *Iphigénie en Tauride* performed at the Burgtheater on 23 October 1781; the abilities of the translator, Johann Baptist von Alxinger, impressed him. In fact, not only was *Iphigenie auf Tauris* scheduled for the autumn, but also a performance in Italian of Gluck's *Alceste*. Mozart reports in the letter of 12 September that although one Gluck work might have opened up a gap for *Idomeneo*, two effectively closed the door in his face. Apart from Mozart's own testimony that he intended Fischer to take the role of Idomeneo, and that Bernasconi and Adamberger were also to be included, any thoughts on a cast-list must be conjectural. Adamberger may well have been intended for Idamante, and Bernasconi for Ilia. Aloysia Lange is another possibility for the latter role, while Caterina Cavalieri would have been more than eligible as Elettra.[31]

Mozart's subsequent endeavours with *Idomeneo* took a slightly different course. At the suggestion of Countess Thun and Adamberger, he began to think of selecting the best numbers for inclusion in concerts (see chapter 2, p. 44, above).[32] In January 1782, he was contemplating works for his forthcoming concert in Lent. The following year, he wrote to his father on 29 March with the programme for his concert that had taken place six days before, including 'Se il padre perdei' performed by Aloysia Lange. Mozart's enthusiasm for a production of *Idomeneo* in what was an increasingly hostile environment for *opera seria* had already waned, however, and in the same letter he told Leopold that he was sending the score of *Idomeneo* back to him in Salzburg.

Vienna 1786

The final chapter in the story of the relationship between Mozart's performers and *Idomeneo* concerns the production at the Auersperg Palace on 13 March 1786. The Auerspergs' private theatre had been used by a professional company between 1776 and 1781, and in 1786 was one of only four private theatres in Vienna.[33] The repertory at the Auersperg theatre included German and French comedies and opera, among them Pergolesi's *La serva padrona* and Grétry's *L'Ami de la maison*. There is no doubt about the casting of major roles (see Table 3.1, p. 49 above). This cast is radically different to those of the Munich or the hypothetical 1781 Vienna productions: the major protagonists were mainly aristocrats and very young. Aristocratic and amateur does not necessarily mean inexperienced, however. Maria Anna Hortensia, Gräfin Hatzfeld, for example, had sung at the Auersperg Palace in Righini's *Armida* in 1782, and in *Alceste* under Gluck's personal direction only a few weeks before *Idomeneo*. A review of the performance in the short-lived periodical *Pfeffer und Salz*, which was in general critical of the work, observed that it succeeded through the merits of Gräfin Hatzfeld's singing – not vice-versa – and suggested her as a rival to Nancy Storace.[34]

The main changes involved recasting the role of Idamante for tenor (Baron Pulini). This entailed rewriting the ensembles and composing the two new numbers entered into Mozart's catalogue three days before the performance: the duet No. 20b and a scena con rondò No. 10b. The latter involved an elaborate accompanied recitative and a substantial instrumental obbligato. Mozart's compositional appetite was now whetted not by the Mannheim woodwind but by his violinist friend Graf August von Hatzfeld, probably Maria Anna's brother-in-law.[35] His skill had been noted by Graf Zinzendorf a year earlier at a performance at the residence of the Gräfin von Thun.[36] The violin writing in Mozart's rondò requires an accomplished soloist in a movement that probes cantabile playing within an andante tempo and bravura passagework in the allegro moderato.

The history of the first performance of *Idomeneo* is in the first instance the history of fitting music to performers, players, and singers who were acquaintances if not firm friends. Its subsequent history is as much the history of fitting players and singers to music. Despite obvious setbacks and failures, especially in Vienna, these experiences stood Mozart in good stead for his work on *Die Entführung aus dem Serail* and the ultimate triumph of the da Ponte operas and *Die Zauberflöte*.

4 *The genre of* Idomeneo

Idomeneo is conveniently referred to in most critical discussions as an *opera seria*. Serious it undoubtedly is; but the genre usually understood by *opera seria* – that against which Gluck and Calzabigi reacted in the dedicatory preface to *Alceste*: a genre consisting mainly of arias, dominated by the singers as much as by the composer and poet – does not supply the framework of *Idomeneo* or even the background from which it departs.[1]

The subtitle on the libretto is 'Dramma per musica', a conventional designation obviously appropriate to a translated *tragédie lyrique* with a happy ending (the designation *opera seria* is in any case comparatively rare in the eighteenth century). 'Dramma per musica' has overtones of very early opera; of this, Mozart certainly knew nothing. He himself referred to *Idomeneo* as 'grosse Opera', a term he does not define, of course, but which he also applied to Holzbauer's *Günther von Schwarzburg*. Ten years later he called Metastasio's *La clemenza di Tito* '*opera seria*' in his personal catalogue, which suggests an understanding of the genre close to the definition offered above. Mozart added that for him *La clemenza* has been 'turned into a real opera'.[2] Its departure from Metastasio takes it closer, but not very close, to *Idomeneo*.

Mozart was well acquainted with the forms and topics of *opera seria*. Before he went to Italy, he met in London one of its leading German exponents, J. C. Bach, who later composed operas for Mannheim and Paris. Mozart's own youthful improvisations in *opera seria* style were described by Daines Barrington.[3] Despite its adherence to what the *Alceste* dedication considered abuses, Italy remained the Mecca of opera-composers, not excluding Gluck. In 1770, almost immediately after arriving in Milan, Mozart was commissioned to write an *opera seria* (*Mitridate, re di Ponto*) for the following carnival. Meanwhile the Mozarts toured Italy and saw operas by, among others, Hasse, Piccinni, and Jommelli. Niccolò

Piccinni was the youngest and most modern in style of these composers; his *Cesare in Egitto* was deemed 'excellent' by Leopold (letter from Milan, 3 February 1770). Wolfgang reported on the dress rehearsal of Niccolò Jommelli's *Armida abbandonata*, which was 'well composed' and which he liked (letter from Naples, 29 May 1770). But his admiration was tempered after the performance, when he called it (5 June) 'beautiful, but too serious and old-fashioned for the theatre'; he also criticised the dances, from an excess of which he was to suffer in Milan, as 'wretchedly pompous'.[4] The magical subject of *Armida* is rather less serious than *Mitridate*, or Mozart's near-masterpiece of conventional *opera seria*, *Lucio Silla* (Milan, 1772). Perhaps Mozart was reacting against musical seriousness, the wealth of orchestration and counterpoint, features for which later, ironically, he himself was criticised.

Idomeneo belongs to a genre cultivated in a number of European centres, which combined the apparently antithetical operatic idioms of France and Italy. This synthesis had been attempted long before the best-remembered 'reform' of opera, that associated with Gluck. In the early 1750s the many articulate Frenchmen who disliked *tragédie lyrique* nevertheless advocated that some of its features – its flexible structure and incorporation of chorus, ballet, and spectacle or 'merveilleux' – should be retained, while the music should be replaced in a modern Italian style freed of irrationalities such as the castrato, overlong ritornellos, and indeed overlong arias and duets.

The contrast between the domain of public affairs and generally agonised, occasionally rapturous, expression of personal feelings is as typical of reform opera as of *opera seria*. The new genre particularly suited subjects in which an individual must be sacrificed for the common benefit; hence Algarotti's choice of *Iphigenia in Aulis* as an ideal subject for reform opera.[5] The reform ideal held that opera should be governed by its poetic idea, not by vocal and instrumental virtuosity. Apart from its Italian libretto and the necessity, in Munich, of giving employment to a castrato, this encyclopaedist ideal, also manifested in Gluck's *Alceste* dedication, lies behind *Idomeneo*.

Mozart's opera clearly represents the mixed French and Italian cultural orientation of Karl Theodor's court, transferred from Mannheim and breaking with the more austere tradition of Munich. The reforming synthesis had already been tried at the Franco-Italian court of Parma, and it appeared at important German centres such as Weimar which, like Mannheim, experimented with 'reform' operas in German by such composers as Anton Schweitzer and Ignaz Holzbauer. Reform operas could co-exist with more traditional forms. Jommelli, for fifteen years Oberkapellmeister at the court of Karl Eugen of Württemburg, set Metastasian *opera seria* alongside French-derived libretti for Stuttgart and Mannheim.[6] The predilections he developed in these operas affected works written after his return to Naples, such as *Armida*. Jommelli's qualifications as a reformer included mastery of the orchestra; he is credited as the inventor, in his opera overtures (sinfonias), of the 'Mannheim crescendo'. His symphonic talent helped him to evoke, as well as accompany, scenes of spectacle; and while he carved out massive aria forms with ample space for vocal virtuosity, he paid exceptional attention even in Metastasian operas to the most expressive part of the form, the obbligato recitatives. He and Verazi also modified such hallowed conventions as the exit aria: their characters may remain on stage after an aria or (at the end of *Ifigenia in Aulide*) even commit suicide. *Idomeneo* is thus partly a continuation of Jommelli's work.

Tommaso Traetta, principal musician of the Parmesan reform, also contributed to the reform tradition. Though his path and Mozart's do not seem to have crossed (he is not mentioned in the family letters), Traetta's *Ippolito ed Aricia*, adapted from a French libretto, was given in Mannheim in 1760 with Dorothea Wendling as Aricia. Conceivably Mozart became aware of Traetta on early visits to Vienna; *Armida* (1761: based on a French libretto) and *Ifigenia in Tauride* (1763, libretto by Marco Coltellini) were both first performed at the Burgtheater.[7]

The evidence suggests that Jommelli and Traetta, both immensely gifted composers, were happy to set whatever poem was set before them; the reforming spirits were the librettists. Gluck owed much to Durazzo, the sympathetic theatre intendant, and his librettist Calzabigi; but like Mozart he later came to control his collaborators. Gluck's genius for musico-dramatic *gesture* was nurtured in his ballets, notably *Don Juan* (1761). The Viennese court had maintained the tradition of involving dance and choral singing in theatrical works (called *azione teatrale*) written for special occasions; but it is hardly necessary to call upon this tradition to explain *Alceste*.[8]

Visiting Vienna in 1767–9, the Mozarts were able to see, as it were in rivalry, Hasse's *opera seria Partenope* and Gluck's *Alceste*, the latter performed by an *opera buffa* troupe on 26 December 1767 (see Leopold's letters of 29 September 1767 and 30 January–

3 February 1768). Although born in the seventeenth century, Hasse was no conservative; his style, like Telemann's, developed to match the newest fashions, bridging the gulf between baroque and classical. Gluck's *Alceste* (Vienna Burgtheater, 1767) marked the first climax (not the instigation) of a reforming ferment. Even at the age of twelve, Mozart must have been struck by the difference between a musically warm but dramatically conventional work like *Partenope* and the icy grandeur and dramatic agonies of *Alceste*, which left a detectable mark on *Don Giovanni* as well as on *Idomeneo*.[9] Jahn noted the resemblance between the High Priests' scenes in *Alceste* and *Idomeneo*, both stirring obbligato recitatives with tremolando accompaniment, punctuated by striding wind arpeggios. Less austere than Gluck, Mozart (No. 23) is scarcely less powerful, substituting a richer harmonic palette for the raw power of Gluck's trombones.[10] Mozart's short version of the oracle (No. 28a) recalls Gluck's laconic voice of Apollo (*Alceste* Act I), though less exactly than does the statue in the graveyard scene of *Don Giovanni*: monotone declamation over shifting wind chords belongs to all three. The 'Fuggiamo' choruses, however, in which the people fly in terror (*Alceste* Act I: *Idomeneo* No. 18), show scarcely any musical likeness.

Another sign of Gluck's example is Mozart's use, for the first time since *Bastien und Bastienne* (1768), of an overture in one movement, articulating conflict by thematic contrast and development. The obvious models, in 1780, were *Alceste* and *Iphigénie en Aulide*, but Mozart does not merely imitate them. Gluck accelerates the tempo in both overtures, and runs them into the first scene, overriding the cadences so that a coda is required for concert performance. Mozart adopted an analogous procedure in *Don Giovanni*; the fading cadence of *Idomeneo* does not go so far. Floros detects Gluck's influence in the high incidence of articulation of harmonic degrees ('Stufen') by pedal-points.[11] But Mozart's structure (see chapter 1, above) is quite unlike Gluck's loose-limbed forms and bespeaks an already experienced symphonist, which Gluck was not.

After his precocious Milan operas, Mozart never returned formally to *opera seria*. This abstinence is probably the result of circumstances rather than preference (Vienna in the 1780s saw hardly any *opera seria*, for Joseph II found it boring). *Lucio Silla* already shows signs of the contemporary reform. The first part of Act I culminates in a fully scored aria in D major (with trumpets and timpani) for the title-role, after which a few bars of ambiguous orchestral harmony cover the scene-change to the tombs of Roman heroes. Cecilio meditates on his plight in a richly orchestrated and harmonically ambitious recitative of a type further developed in *Idomeneo*. He has no aria; the music flows into a chorus, the middle section of which is a solo for Giunia (compare 'Placido è il mar'); and the mingling of ritualistic chorus and solo in a larger structural unit (Nos. 24 and 26) is characteristic of Traetta as well as Gluck. No later scene in this creakingly plotted opera lives up to this; and *Lucio Silla* remains an aria-dominated *opera seria*. Table 4.1 compares the disposition of aria forms in *Idomeneo* with a classic libretto, *La clemenza di Tito*, Jommelli's traditionally formed *Armida*, and Mozart's own *Lucio Silla*. *Idomeneo*'s fourteen arias bring it nearly into line with the da Ponte comedies, although no aria in *Idomeneo* is short or song-like. However, the actual total of arias in *Idomeneo* performances may have been as low as ten.

Table 4.1

Title	Prima donna	Primo uomo	Primo tenore	Seconda donna	Secondo uomo	Other
La clemenza di Tito	Vitellia	Sesto	Tito	Servilia	Annio	Publio
	5	5	4	5	4	1
Armida	Armida	Rinaldo	Tancredi	Erminia	Rambaldo	Dano, Ubaldo
	4 + duet	4 + duet	3	2	3	1 each
Lucio Silla	Giunia	Cecilio	Silla	Celia	Cinna	Aufidio
	4	4	2	4	3	1
Idomeneo	Ilia	Idamante	Idomeneo	Elettra	none	Arbace
	3	3	3	3		2

Note: 'Uomo' signifies castrato. I have not included the ensembles in *Idomeneo*; for a full distribution, see Table 7.1, p. 97, below. *La clemenza* is Metastasio's text, not the version set by Mozart.

In 1775 Mozart wrote a remarkably mature lachrymose comedy, *La finta giardiniera*, for Munich, and a version of Metastasio's *Il re pastore* for Salzburg. Two years later he went by way of Mannheim to Paris, a disastrous trip from many points of view – his love for Aloysia Weber was not returned; his mother died in Paris; he composed little – but one which bore artistic fruit in the long run. In Mannheim he saw Ignaz Holzbauer's earnest German opera *Günther von Schwarzburg*.[12] Mozart disliked the libretto, poorly motivated and full of nationalistic swagger ('The poetry doesn't deserve such music'), but commended the beauty and fire of the composition (letter of 14 November 1777). He presumably admired the continuity by which arias are merged into the wealth of obbligato recitatives; these features reappear in *Idomeneo*, written for the same orchestra and some of the same singers. Holzbauer's musical training was thoroughly Italian, but he turned virtuosic vocal writing to dramatic effect. The spitfire Queen Asberta has been compared to the Queen of Night, but Elettra comes just as strongly to mind.[13] Holzbauer prefigures other aspects of *Idomeneo*, using the chief idea of an aria during the preceding orchestral recitative (cf. R. 13, R. 19), and including flute and oboe solos, presumably for Wendling and Ramm, in an aria for Raaff.[14]

In Paris Mozart may have heard the most recent French operas by Gluck, *Iphigénie en Aulide* (1774), the revised *Alceste* (1776), and *Armide* (1777). He certainly heard Piccinni's first French opera, *Roland*; and this, with its grateful lyricism married to a French libretto, is the most recent model for *Idomeneo*. Mozart came to dislike typically French music, and in *Roland* he may have seen an acceptable synthesis on which to build. Piccinni's music itself is too bland to have interested Mozart much, and he told Leopold that 'I can do as well as his Piccinni – although I am only a German'.[15]

Mozart wrote one other opera before *Idomeneo*, the aborted Singspiel *Zaide*. Under the spell of the melodramas *Medea* and *Ariadne auf Naxos* by Georg Benda, Mozart said that 'most operatic recitatives should be treated this way' (letter of 12 November 1778), as speech punctuated, and occasionally backed, by expressive music.[16] In *Zaide* he put this theory into practice and the experience of writing melodrama surely contributed to the expressiveness of the *Idomeneo* recitatives. In particular the first melodrama has a richness of harmony and an expressiveness of motivic invention which even the best *Idomeneo* recitatives hardly surpass. The choruses of *Idomeneo* may also owe less to the obvious operatic model, Gluck, than to Mozart's own recent experience: nearly contemporary with *Zaide*, the incidental music for *Thamos, König in Ägypten* contains both melodramas and fine choruses which anticipate *Idomeneo* and *Die Zauberflöte*. Since *Thamos* was intended for Salzburg, Mozart also used, presumably, the identical trumpet mutes later sent to Munich for *Idomeneo*.

Idomeneo was an adventure by an experienced composer into a continuing, though not very ancient, tradition. Mozart was certainly up to date in his knowledge of contemporary opera, and eager to conform to the expectations of the Mannheim entourage, now translated to Munich, for an opera which combined Italian lyricism with French flexibility of design and a richness of colouring which it would be anachronistic to call symphonic: it, too, is really the outcome of Franco-Gluckist development. There is nothing revolutionary about the structure of *Idomeneo*, which was also anticipated in many details. Much the same, of course, could be said of *Le nozze di Figaro*. Mozart's originality seldom appears in the clothing of his ideas; it lies rather in the subtlety of musical language which enables him to create in the listener the illusion that he has penetrated within the minds of the characters.

5   *From myth to libretto*

The mythological background

JULIAN RUSHTON

The story of Idomeneus is scantily represented in mythology and literature. Its comparative popularity in the eighteenth century may have something to do with a desire vicariously to stage the story of Jephtha, at a time when biblical subjects were generally banned from the theatre. Jephtha's daughter, like Idamante (and, in a far more widely known Greek tale, Iphigenia), is willing to die at her father's hand:

And Jephtha vowed a vow unto the Lord, and said, If thou shalt without fail deliver the children of Ammon into mine hands, Then it shall be that whatsoever cometh forth of the doors of my house to meet me, when I return in peace from the children of Ammon, shall surely be the Lord's, and I will offer it up as a burnt offering . . . behold, his daughter came out to meet him with timbrels and with dances; and she was his only child; And it came to pass, when he saw her, that he rent his clothes, and said, Alas, my daughter! thou hast brought me very low, and thou art one of them that trouble me: for I have opened my mouth unto the Lord, and I cannot go back. And she said unto him: My father, if thou hast opened thy mouth unto the Lord, do to me according to that which hath proceeded out of thy mouth; forasmuch as the Lord hath taken vengeance for thee of thine enemies, even the children of Ammon.[1]

In the earliest versions of the Jephtha, Idomeneus, and Agamemnon stories the sacrifice is consummated. However, an escape from such a bitter ending goes back at least to Euripides (*Iphigenia in Aulis*), and was generally preferred in the later eighteenth century, which nevertheless continued to regard Euripides as 'extrêmement tragique'.[2]

Idomeneus was a Greek chieftain whose kingdom of Crete figures in mythology through the legends of Minos, Theseus, Ariadne, and the Minotaur, and in archaeology for the great Minoan palaces which may have given rise to these stories. But if Idomeneus existed he was vassal and ally to the Great King of Mycenae. Modern versions of his story moved his capital from inland Knossos to the port of Kydonia (Sidon). He belongs to Mycenaean civilisation, not the earlier Minoan phase. On an early statue, his escutcheon bore a cockerel (so the familiar Minoan emblems, bulls' horns, are not appropriate to *Idomeneo*).[3] Hyginus mentions him among Helen's suitors; Homer gives him eighty black-sailed ships, and includes him among the heroes who volunteered to take on Hector in single combat. Apollodorus and Lycophron, perhaps by analogy with Agamemnon, have his wife Meda committing adultery with his regent Leucus.[4]

None of the major Greek authors mentions the tradition of his fatal vow and the sacrifice of his son, which belongs structurally with other 'home-coming vow' stories.[5] Virgil mentions Idomeneus' banishment from Crete, without explanation; but his commentator Servius Honaratus describes the storm at sea and the vow to Neptune, leaving open the question whether Idomeneus actually carried out the sacrifice.[6] The origin of modern treatments of the subject is the didactic romance *Télémaque* (1699) by François de la Mothe-Fénelon (1651–1715), a pioneer of Enlightenment whom Leopold Mozart admired, enough to visit his grave in 1766; Wolfgang himself began to read *Télémaque* in 1770.[7]

Well before Fénelon, it had become normal to assume that Idomeneus was a Minoan, son of Deucalion and thus grandson of Minos. In Fénelon's Book V, Telemachus learns that Crete, far from being the ferocious and decadent society of the Theseus legend, is an earthly paradise: as in Homeric sources Minos (a son of Zeus who became a judge in the underworld) bound himself by his own laws and ruled for the general good as a father to his people. When Telemachus lands, he hears of Idomeneus' banishment. Fénelon's account of the vow resembles all later treatments. Then we hear that Idomeneus, soon after landing, tried to substitute an animal sacrifice, was driven mad by Nemesis, and killed his son.[8] In exile, Idomeneus founds a new enlightened kingdom at Salente in Italy, where he is visited by Telemachus (Books VIII–XI).

The immediate source used by Mozart's librettist Gianbattista Varesco was a *tragédie lyrique* by Antoine Danchet, based in turn on a neo-classical verse tragedy. Iphigenia, the other child-sacrifice from the Trojan War, was represented in French tradition by *Iphigénie en Aulide*, one of the most popular of Racine's tragedies; it had no French operatic treatment until 1774 (Gluck), but there were some Italian operas on the subject, one (by Galuppi) staged in Rome three weeks before the birth of Mozart.[9] Danchet's source was by a lesser author than Racine: *Idoménée* (1705) marked the theatrical debut of Prosper Jolyot de Crébillon (1674–1762; see below, p. 73), whose inspiration was surely Racine. The subject reappeared in the unsuccessful tragedy by A.-M. Lemierre (1764) who, unlike Crébillon, adopted the operatic convention of using several locations, and also relates the subject to the Iphigenia legend by referring to the custom of human sacrifice in Tauris. In Lemierre the son (named Idamante by Crébillon) is already married. As in Crébillon, he stabs himself to spare his father, and the king goes into voluntary exile. Clearly this version was unknown, or of no interest, to Varesco.[10]

In mythology, the characters of Mozart's operas are either shadowy, like Idomeneus, or nameless, like his son. Danchet, however, made both his female characters interesting by devising a pre-history for them. He named Ilione (Ilia) after Ilios (Troy).[11] No author before Danchet associates Electra, the only character drawn from true mythology, with Crete. She is best-known as a child of Agamemnon who remained in Argos through all the troubles, culminating in the murder of Clytemnestra by Orestes. If she were exiled after the murder of Agamemnon, it would have been immediately after the war; she could, thus, have preceded Iliona and Idomeneus to Crete, and set her cap at Idamante. Curiously enough, Ilia (in R. 1) and Elettra herself in 'D'Oreste, d'Aiace' imply that she is escaping after the murder of Clytemnestra; taken literally, this would mean that Idomeneus, like Odysseus, spent many years getting home. This is probably a careless anachronism.

Arbace, a confidant with at least one aria too many, requires no comment. The High Priest of Neptune aroused the ire of Dent, who noted that he 'takes no part in [the final] scene; after the capitulation of the oracle – no doubt stage-managed by himself – he probably thinks it would be more prudent to keep out of the way'. But the pressure exerted by the priest on the king (No. 23) does not make him a sinister figure like Calchas in *Iphigénie en Aulide*, who knows the victim's name and is thus able to manipulate Agamemnon. Less malevolent than his prototype in Danchet, Neptune's priest in Mozart's opera prays for the sacrifice to be remitted (No. 24); why should he not consider the sacrifice, even of the king's son, a high price which must nevertheless be exacted for the safety of the whole population?[12]

From *tragédie lyrique* to moral drama

DON NEVILLE

Much of the *Idomeneo* libretto is a translation, by Gianbattista Varesco, of Antoine Danchet's *Idomenée*, a text set by André Campra (1660–1744) and first performed in Paris in 1712. Danchet (1671–1748) began both his collaboration with Campra and his career as a stage writer with *Vénus*, a *fête galante* performed privately in January 1698. The Danchet–Campra team then produced several pastorales, ballets and *opéra ballets* between 1698 and 1735, in addition to eleven *tragédies lyriques* that included *Hésione* (1700), *Tancrède* (1702), *Télémaque* (1704), and *Idomenée* (1712). Danchet became a member of the Académie française in the year of *Idomenée*, and its director from 1727. Although he wrote four spoken tragedies, these works were never to achieve the acclaim accorded to his *livrets* written for the musical theatre.

The Trojan Wars and the wrath of Venus incurred by any who fought against Troy provide the fundamental motivating forces behind the action of Danchet's *tragédie*. Venus/Aphrodite, having been declared the most beautiful of all the goddesses by Paris, son of King Priam of Troy, aided him in abducting Helen, wife of Sparta's King Menelaus. Danchet begins with a prologue in which Venus calls upon Aeolus, god of the winds, to unleash a storm that will prevent Idomenée from reaching the shores of Crete. The first act begins as King Priam's daughter, Ilione, a prisoner on Crete and the beloved of Idomenée himself, tells Dircé, her confidante, that she is falling in love with the king's son Idamante, but fears that he also has the love of Agamemnon's daughter, Electre, who is in Crete. Idamante enters, a prey to two different emotions, love for Ilione and concern for the safety of his father. He announces that he will free all the Trojan prisoners, and a divertissement follows, performed by the Cretan women and the Trojan soldiers. News comes that Idomenée has perished in a storm. Idamante is devastated, and Ilione, too, mourns the passing of a hero. Electre sees this as the death of her hope that Idamante will return her love, since he is now free to marry Ilione. Furious, she determines to be revenged.

Act II begins with a terrible storm. Neptune quells it and demands from Idomenée, now safely on shore, the fulfilment of his promise to sacrifice the first person he sees in gratitude for his delivery. Idomenée contemplates in horror the prospect of shedding innocent blood. Arriving with an offer of help for the unknown ship-wrecked nobleman, Idamante is overjoyed to discover that it is his father, and cannot understand why Idomenée flies from him in despair. Meanwhile, Electre calls upon Venus to avenge her unrequited love. In a second divertissement, the goddess summons the Cupids and Jealousy (La Jalousie) to be the instruments of her vengeance.

As Act III begins, Idomenée rails against Neptune and Venus, and conspires to avert destiny by sending Idamante back to Argos as escort to Electre. Alone, after confessing to Ilione his love for her, he admits to being ashamed of his actions and emotions, but powerless to change them. Electre, delighted with Idomenée's plan, views the voyage as an opportunity to pursue her interest in Idamante. A divertissement follows. As Idamante and Electre are about to embark, a tempest suddenly arises, and Proteus (Protée), Neptune's herdsmen, calls up a monster out of the sea. Idomenée defies the gods and offers himself as victim, refusing to sacrifice his son.

Act IV takes place in the temple of Neptune. Dircé tells Ilione that Idamante is to do battle with the sea monster. Rejected by his father, scorned by his beloved, Idamante is determined to die to save his people. Ilione confesses her love, but tells him she is loved by his father also. Idomenée enters, and orders everyone to leave the temple so that he may pray alone to Neptune. Idamante's victory over the monster is announced, and a divertissement of rejoicing ensues.

Act V begins propitiously. Idomenée abdicates in favour of Idamante and permits his marriage to Ilione. Electre, however, still seeks revenge, and her prayer brings a response from the gods. As the abdication is being celebrated, Nemesis strikes Idomenée with such hallucinations that he kills Idamante. Upon regaining his sanity, he prepares to take his own life, but Ilione insists that he live as punishment; she herself must die.

Much of the action that Danchet has superimposed on the classical story was suggested by Crébillon who, in addition to the classical sources, had also drawn upon the account in Fénelon's *Télémaque*. Crébillon retained the references to the shipwreck, the vow to Neptune, and the meeting between father and son, and introduced, as items of dramatic significance, the general sufferings inflicted by the infuriated gods, the preparations for the sacrifice, and the oracle. As was normal in operatic adaptations of French neo-classical dramas, Danchet makes visible on stage such vital moments in the action as the shipwreck and the initial meeting between father and son. He replaced Crébillon's references to the scourges sent by the gods with actual appearances of Proteus and the sea monster, shows Neptune calming the waves, and Jealousy, personified, agreeing to possess Idomenée. He is also responsible for the added complexity of Electre's presence, for her fury upon hearing the false news of Idomenée's death (itself a Danchet addition), and for the response of Venus to her appeal for vengeance. Finally, Danchet replaced Erixène, daughter of an enemy usurper, with Ilione, daughter of Priam himself; and he reworked the ending.[13]

In transforming Danchet's *livret* into a libretto for Mozart, Varesco deleted the prologue and recast the five-act *tragédie lyrique* as a three-act *dramma musicale*. His first act incorporates most of Danchet's Acts I and II, and his second act parallels Danchet's Act III. Varesco's Act III then follows most of Danchet's Act IV up to the point of the announcement that Idamante has slain the sea monster, whereupon the two texts diverge towards their different conclusions. Varesco removed Danchet's five divertissements, one from each act, retaining only elements of them in the *pantomima* and ballet in Act I, the brief supernatural manifestations in Acts II and III, and the final ballet. Two other deletions involved characters. Dircé, Ilone's confidante, was removed, and much of the original dialogue between these two characters became soliloquy for Varesco's Ilia. Arcas, Idomenée's confidant, was combined with Arbas, Idamante's attendant to create the Arbace of *Idomeneo*. Finally, Varesco removed one of Danchet's most significant additions derived from Crébillon, the rivalry in love between Idomenée and Idamante, but expanded the recognition scene between father and son as well as adding to the preparation for sacrifice with the insertion of three scenes for Idomeneo to explain his procrastination.

Varesco, in making these alterations, changed the emphasis of Danchet's drama in two fundamental ways. First, he turned a French *tragédie lyrique*, with appropriate Aristotelian foundations, into a moral drama along Metastasian lines for which the principles of Aristotle had long since been reinterpreted. Secondly, in performing this task, he considerably lowered the level of supernatural influence evident in Danchet's plot, thus transferring greater dramatic significance to the action at the human level while simultaneously removing much of the motivation for this action. That the conversion process also created problems for the composer is yet another issue.

Idomenée is destroyed through direct confrontation with supernatural powers; indeed, his fate is predetermined by divinities who constantly and visibly manoeuvre the action. In the impressive opening to *Idomenée*, Venus and Neptune unite their powers to wreak vengeance against the king of Crete for his part in the sack of Troy, and their victory provides the dramatic conclusion. Between the beginning and end, intermittent appearances of these and related divinities (Act II, Scenes 1–2; Act II, Scenes 5–8; Act III, Scenes 7–8) serve as visible reminders of their absolute power, against which all mortal endeavour is futile. As in Sophocles' *Oedipus Rex*, one of two models often cited by Aristotle, the fate of the title character is sealed from the outset, and retaliatory suffering is imposed by the gods upon a city for an offence unknown to its populace. Men of good fortune are brought to ill-fortune, the tragic acts involve close kindred of high rank, the perpetrator is unaware of his victim's identity at the time of performing these acts, and recognition follows with the appropriate pitiful show of remorse.

As a part imitator of a Greek model, Danchet was obliged to show a certain deference to moral content. In Act II, Scene 4, for example, Idamante assures the as yet unrecognised stranger on the shore that:

Le seul plaisir de vous défendre	The mere pleasure of helping you
Suffira pour combler mes vœux:	Is enough to fulfil my desires:

Idomenée, almost overcome by jealousy of his son in Act III, Scene 3, exclaims:

Jaloux ressentiment,	Jealous resentment,
loin de vous écouter,	far from heeding you
Je dois rougir	I ought to blush
d'une honteuse flamme.	with a shameful passion.

Near the end of Act IV, Idomenée renounces all claim on Ilione with the words:

En unissant mon fils	In uniting my son
à l'objet de ses vœux,	with the object of his desires,
Faisons céder l'Amant au Père.	Let us make the lover yield to the father.

Such attention to moral utterance and example for Danchet, however, was a side issue. For the Metastasian-style moral drama, it was the essence that could quite overthrow the basic premise of Greek tragedy that the central character be cast down through direct confrontation with superior powers. Instead, Metastasio consciously barred such 'barbarity' from his dramas, pointing out that the virtues of a Hercules or a Theseus, as depicted by an ancient writer, are usually violent, unjust, dissolute, rash, bloody, and cruel, and are in no way analogous to 'quegli abiti ragionevoli dell'animo, che noi reputiamo ora unicamente degni del nome di virtù' (those reasonable ways of the soul that we now consider uniquely deserving the name of virtue).[14]

For the moral drama, action meant moral action in which the characters display human emotions born of the strength or weakness of their moral standing. The dominant moral virtues, moral failings, and overriding passions of the characters are selected according to the moral aims of the plot. The action will then unfold with probability if the author ensures that the virtues and emotions respond according to the expectations laid down by a moral code familiar to a particular society at a particular period in time. The conflicts are moral conflicts, and the characters are moral types, animated by their moral trials, the consequence of errors in moral judgements, or by failings in their pursuit of virtue. Moral reason holds pride of place over impulsive behaviour, and morality demands its own reward in an obligatory happy ending, made particularly meaningful if the central moral hero draws the less morally strong to a realisation of moral truth.

In place of the all-powerful gods, Varesco opens *Idomeneo* with a *scena* for the vulnerable Ilia, and typically, her opening lines proclaim a state of emotional agitation already aroused:

Quando avran fine omai	When will my bitter misfortunes
l'aspre sventure mie?	have an end?
Ilia infelice!	Unhappy Ilia!

The moral dilemma is articulated soon afterwards, ending in a Metastasian turn of phrase:

Ah, qual contrasto, oh Dio!	Ah, what conflict, o god!
d'opposti affetti	of opposing desires
Mi destate nel sen,	You arouse in my breast,
odio ed amore!	hatred and love!
Vendetta deggio a chi	I owe vengeance to him
mi diè la vita,	who gave me life,
Gratitudine a chi	Gratitude to him
vita mi rende . . .	who saved my life . . .

Similarly, in Idamante's reply to Elettra when she chides him for freeing the Trojan prisoners, the impression is Metastasian even if the poetic style is not:

Veder basti all Grecia	It is enough for the Greeks
Vinto il nemico.	To see the enemy conquered.
Opra di me più degna	Prepare yourself, O Princess,
A mirar s'apparecchi,	To behold a deed more
o principessa;	worthy of me;
Vegga il vinto felice.	Let us see the vanquished happy.

Danchet was satisfied with:

Princesse, c'est assez	Princess, it is enough
de les avoir soumis,	to have subdued them,
Leur bonheur sera	Their welfare will be my task.
mon ouvrage.	

Varesco already had a moral hero in Idamante who would set free his enemies, display filial love and duty, risk his life and eventually yield himself as a sacrifice for the sake of his people. He would also draw Ilia from her state of dilemma to the 'right' decision, absolve his father's obligation to the gods, and win their approval as king. A virtuous Idomeneo was, therefore, not essential. Yet, although turning the king from Ilia's lover to her father figure, Varesco was still able to treat him, if not as a Metastasian 'offender', at least as one who, having committed one major act of folly, is thrown into a moral dilemma (satisfy the gods or save his son) which is then compounded (to propitiate the gods is to sacrifice Ilia also) until appropriate confession and final trial lead to absolution.

Whatever were the demands placed upon Varesco from Munich, they essentially enforced upon him the unenviable task of imposing the requirements of moral drama as overlay upon a trimmed *Idomenée*.[15] Such a graft was difficult, and it is not surprising to find the attempt accused of being 'verbose and sententious', to which 'hyperbolic' might also be added.[16] Metastasio was a proven master in the art of poetic lyricism, delicate nuance, and emotional poignancy through the direct and economical manipulation of language. The tendency of an imitator to exaggerate fundamental traits of the moral drama and to inflate the basic style is rather to be expected.

Along with Varesco's deletion of the prologue went the removal of Venus as the prime mover against Idomeneo. In Danchet's text, she is the dominating deity who joins forces with other divinities, one of whom is Neptune, to destroy the royal line of Crete.[17] It is Venus who divides father and son by arranging the storm that spawns the vow of sacrifice, and who enlists the aid of Jealousy to separate the two as rivals in love. It is Venus also who gives strength and substance to the demands of Electre for vengeance, and who orchestrates the final catastrophe. With her removal, along with several other deities and primal forces, are lost the momentous actions that link directly to a vengeance born out of the epic proportions of the Trojan Wars. Only Neptune remains, his lesser and far weaker motive for anger in *Idomeneo* being that of a single unfulfilled vow.

The image of Troy's destruction remains, of course, as part of Ilia's dilemma. Here, however, the matter is one of temporary moral obstacle, not a driving force towards catastrophe. Elettra, whose equivalent in Danchet's text is integrated with the vengeance process as a mortal suppliant on its behalf, becomes but an enraged and jealous bystander in the Varesco version. Finally, the elimination of the supernaturally induced love of Idomeneo for Ilia both simplifies the king's emotions and reduces the menace he represents for her. As products of supernatural possession, Idomenée's sudden displays of animosity towards Ilione or outbursts against his son stem from powers beyond his control. Such explosive behaviour is consistent with his hasty vow to Neptune, his subsequent cries against the god, his defiance, and his brusque rebuttals of Idamante. As stated in Danchet's Act II, Scene 3, this character not only fears Venus and Neptune, but also himself, and with good reason. With an Idomeneo reacting only in response to a need to shield his son, motivation for much of his former erratic behaviour is lost, together with certain of the magnitude and rudimentary ruggedness of his original counterpart.

For Ilia, the removal of Idomeneo's fateful love leaves her challenged only by the inner conflict between love and honour which she expresses at the outset of the opera. That Idamante becomes a figure of opposition is entirely her own doing, a matter which she takes two acts to resolve, during which time she is faced with the possibility of his departure and death (in combat with the monster). There is no surprise in her capitulation, since its likelihood is already suggested in the opening text, within the musical content of the first aria, and picked up again in the second and sixth scenes of Act II.[18] In place of the heated confrontation between Idomeneo and Ilia in Danchet's Act III, Scene 2 is Varesco's Act II,

Scene 2, a most congenial scene of minimal dramatic tension. Another gentle aria follows for Ilia at the beginning of Varesco's Act III, an aria in which the dilemma of Act I is seen to have been considerably diluted by strengthened affections for Idamante. The following love duet is inevitable, and the lovers are left undisturbed by extraneous concerns. Again a dramatically weaker situation than Danchet's Act IV, Scenes 1 and 3, in which tension is generated through fears of Idoménee's interference as rival to his son. Vengeance for the sack of Troy, the original 'cause' of Venus transferred to Ilia, has in the end to be suppressed so that her final reconciliation with Idamante can satisfy the typical requirement of moral drama that faithful love be rewarded. Further, as distinct from the Ilione of *Idoménée*, the Ilia of *Idomeneo* is driven by only one basic concern, and once this has been expressed in Act I, Scene 1 the text offers her little chance to display the mettle of her emotional fibre until her challenge of the sacrifice at the end of the opera.

From the viewpoint of motivation and its effect upon character portrayal, Idamante, in comparison to the other three main characters, is transferred from Danchet to Varesco almost unchanged. A victim of his father's vow, of Ilia's sense of honour, and of Elettra's adoration, he also assumes the role of possible victim to the monster, taking upon himself the eradication of the source of Sidon's miseries.

In all, the scope of the issues that motivate plot and character in *Idoménée* has been reduced in *Idomeneo*, resulting in less dramatic tension and less complexity in the story line. The simpler characters are each propelled by a singularity of motive, acting with greater restraint and refinement along lines which would have been acceptable to courtly *buon gusto* or *la bienséance*. With a limited number of actions to be extended across three acts of a drama by characters of restricted dimensions, the role of the chorus, consideration of pace, and the manipulation of contrast become particularly vital.

The reduction of supernatural interferences in *Idomeneo* increases the emphasis upon the human elements – upon the interaction and reactions of the dramatis personae and their problematic moral obligations. Having replaced the gods with an opening that focuses upon Ilia and her moral conflict, Varesco then reduced Neptune's role in the shipwreck (Act I, Scenes 7–8), thus directing more attention towards Idomeneo and his predicament. Similarly, the addition of the trio at the end of Act II (No. 16) and the deletion of the pronouncement of Proteus add weight to the human element at the expense of the deities, even though the sea monster still appears. The same applies to the reduction of all supernatural intervention at the end of the drama to a mere subterranean voice, reduced, in one Mozart version, to nine bars (No. 28a). Here are tested Idomeneo's choice between filial love and kingly duty, Idamante's choice between love for an individual and patriotic devotion, and Ilia's ultimate capacity for self-sacrificial love. The essential emphasis of *Idomeneo*, the moral drama, is not that of *Idomenée*, the more Aristotelian *tragédie lyrique*, even if much of the text is the same.

Along with this shift in emphasis came a conscious interest in realism, a subject that recurs in the Mozart correspondence written during the time of the opera's composition in Munich. There are discussions over Idomeneo's arrival with or without followers (letters on 13 and 18 November, and 22 December 1780); the length of the recognition scene (Act I, Scene 10; 19, 22, and 27 December); the replacement of an aria in Act II, Scene 6 with an obbligato recitative (13 and 18 November); the addition of a march in Act III, and the deletion of Elettra's final aria to avoid awkward exits and re-entries (3 January 1781). Similarly, an inserted scene for Arbace (Act III, Scene 5) and a change of location (Act III, Scenes 6–7) add a degree of credence to Idamante's slaying of the monster, considering that he departs in Act III, Scene 4, and does not return until the end of Act III, Scene 7. Danchet has no change of scene, and his Idamante has killed the monster by the end of Act IV, Scene 5, having only departed at the end of Act IV, Scene 4, necessitating only the briefest of combats and a monster ready at hand.

Danchet's *tragédie lyrique* has a prologue and five acts that involve more characters in more complex situations than are found in Varesco's three-act drama. In what remains, the variety of character-motivations that have to support the action has been considerably reduced and weakened. Varesco, however, wrote almost as many lines as Danchet, and his third act, where Varesco was called upon to do his most original work, is nearly as long as the other two acts combined. The extended musical forms of Italian opera replaced the concise lyrical moments of the French form, and although both works have similar quantities of recitative, *Idomeneo* contains four times the amount of slow-moving obbligato recitative than is found in *Idomenée*. Indeed, if all the music that Mozart wrote for the 1781 *Idomeneo* were to be used, the three-act opera would take longer to perform than its counterpart with prologue and five acts. The problem of how to manipulate less material over a longer time span was a real one, as Mozart's deletions to the score even before the opera's first performance will attest. Individually, Mozart's ingredients are exquisitely expressive, but collectively, they add to the problems of pace already inherent in the text.

The opera's exposition, for example, takes almost the entire first act. With Danchet's prologue gone, Ilia must provide a great deal of essential information at the outset. This done, Idamante and Elettra give separate utterance to their problems in Act I, Scene 2 and Act I, Scene 6, but it is not until Act I, Scene 9 and Act I, Scene 10, however, that the entry of the title role and his meeting with his son identifies the most fundamental conflict of the plot. The text for Ilia's opening scene is shorter than its French equivalent but, set almost entirely in obbligato recitative, its delivery is much slower. For the remaining expository scenes, both the texts and their settings are longer in the Italian opera than the French, with music's role considerably expanded in the former. Like Mozart, Campra also uses *récitatif obligé* in his Electre scene (Act I, Scene 6) but with eight lines and eighteen bars as opposed to Mozart's fifteen lines and forty-four bars. Further, in Act I, Scene 1, Campra's air of fourteen bars is matched by the 115 bars of 'Padre, germani'; in Act I, Scene 2 an air/duet of thirty-two bars compares with the 150 bars of Idamante's 'Non ho colpa', and in Act I, Scene 6, an air of sixty-eight bars for Electre stands where the 151 bars of Elettra's 'Tutte nel cor vi sento' occur in Mozart's score.

With the elongation of the units that produce the 'intense seriousness' and 'monumental strength' of *Idomeneo*, the overall dramatic impact of the opera becomes particularly dependent upon the element of contrast.[19] The chorus numbers, even those that do not add to the progress of the plot, are vital elements in this respect as are the manifestations of the supernatural, upon which the plot still depends in spite of the accents on realism and personal human drama. If the supernatural aspects are underplayed, the monster at the end of Act II and the voice that brings about the *lieto fine* remain distanced from the remainder of the action. The ever-present threat of the sea, a visual effect called for in the scene descriptions, helps to align these occult elements with the human action. So also do the *pantomima* of Act I, Scene 8 and the marine ballet of the 'Intermezzo' wherein the awesome omnipresence of the gods is emphasised and their mystic world acknowledged in dance. The effect of the contrasts in the first half of the Mozart–Varesco Act III, for example, is weakened if all Mozart's vocal music for the second half is retained and the ballet deleted. In order to maintain a strong dramatic rhythm, the long, quiet opening, the mounting tension of the expected sacrifice, and the unexpected revocation need to find immediate release in the broad spectacle of the final chorus and ballet, as was apparently Mozart's preference for the première.

Idomeneo, the final product of the conversion from French *livret* to realised Italian opera, approached, in content, the Metastasian moral drama, the quintessential model for the *opera seria* or *dramma per musica*. It retained, however, sufficient traits of its Gallic origin to create neither a *tragédie lyrique* nor, entirely, an *opera seria*, but a hybrid created from the two. If such a creation still requires classification, surely the most appropriate has been assigned by Mozart himself: 'grosse Opera'.[20]

6 Idomeneo *after Mozart*

Into the nineteenth century

JULIAN RUSHTON

After the three Munich performances, Mozart tried to pave the way for a Viennese production by performing parts of *Idomeneo* at concerts. But the end of the National Singspiel and the engagement of an *opera buffa* troupe effectively barred the way to *Idomeneo* at the Burgtheater, whether in Italian or, as Mozart probably intended, in German. The single 1786 performance was in a private theatre;[1] the first public Vienna production, which was in German, came only in 1806.[2]

There seem to have been no performances of *Idomeneo* during the 1790s, but Mozart's posthumously growing fame led to a spate of publications, including plans for issuing his complete works. Three vocal scores of *Idomeneo* were published in 1797–8, and in 1800 the overture appeared in the popular domestic form of a piano duet. The full score was first published by Simrock in 1805 (entitled *Idomeneo ossia Ilia ed Idamante*). Other vocal scores appeared throughout the century, and in 1868 Breitkopf and Härtel initiated a series of operatic full scores with *Idomeneo*. International interest is evident from the publication of vocal scores in London and Paris in 1811, not apparently related to performances.[3]

Most productions were in German, the first in 1802 at Kassel.[4] *Idomeneo*'s French origins are reflected in a strange production in Paris, described as with 'words by M. Caigniez, arranged from the opera by Mozart by J. L. Bertin', in 1822. The cast included confidantes for Idamante and Ilia, but Elettra disappears, her first aria being incongruously transferred to Ilia (Ilione). Neptune publicly announces the need for a sacrifice; nevertheless, when Idamante and Idomeneo meet, they have enough sang-froid to sing a duet.[5] In

83

the same year a piano score was published in Paris by Schlesinger, with Italian text; however, a fully staged performance of a relatively authentic version did not take place in Paris until 1933.[6]

According to Otto Jahn, who began his major biography in the centenary of Mozart's birth, *Idomeneo* 'has been given from time to time on different stages, without exciting as much interest in the general public as the better-known works of Mozart; the judgment of connoisseurs, on the other hand, has always distinguished it'.[7] The subsequent history of *Idomeneo*, a series of discrete revivals rather than assimilation into the repertory, bears out the truth of this observation. Publication allowed *Idomeneo* to become an object of serious critical attention, and the beginnings of a modern critical view are to be found in a review of the Simrock full score by the composer and journalist J. F. Reichardt.

By no means a Mozart worshipper, Reichardt nevertheless placed *Idomeneo* on a pedestal: it is 'a work . . . which fulfils all our wishes . . . The purest work of art which our Mozart himself ever completed . . .'[8] Reichardt praised the characterisation in detail, attributing that of the High Priest, and the choruses, to the example of Gluck. The work is 'throughout of pure sustained heroic character, without alloy', despite the admittedly Italian nature of several arias: a more balanced view than some which followed of what, for Mozart, represents a pure style. In the first book about the operas (1848), Mozart's biographer A. D. Ulybyshev attempted to discriminate between the influences of *opera seria* and of Gluck and French opera. Like most early historical assessments, however, this fails sufficiently to consider the repertory of Mannheim.[9] Such discussions of influence (which continue to the present day) tend to make *Idomeneo* appear more uneven than it really is. After Reichardt's generation, general knowledge of the unreformed *opera seria* sharply declined, and music so much more conspicuously grateful for voices than Gluck's (whose operas were still well known) could be mistaken for mere singers' opera. Jahn identified French influence on the choruses and recitative (yet in the passage 'Già regna la morte' (No. 24) he found that 'the intensity and almost over-wealth of beauty . . . give the music . . . the national stamp of the Italian opera'). He considered the women's arias original, but saw Mozart as fettered by the Italian tradition which nurtured Panzacchi, dal Prato, and Raaff, whose 'bravura passages . . . are completely obsolete'. Elsewhere, however, 'the impulse of German art laid hold . . . of his innermost being, and gave him clear consciousness of his capabilities as a German artist'.[10]

In 1879 Eduard Hanslick, reviewing the first Vienna performance for sixty years, echoes this view of *Idomeneo* as a work of intermittent genius and elevated sentiment, but intolerably mixed quality and style.[11] He distinguishes it sharply from Mozart's later operas, praising the 'Shakespearian' mixture of comedy and tragedy in *Don Giovanni* at the expense of *Idomeneo*; in Mozart's time Hanslick's comparison to Corneille and Racine would have been interpreted as favourable to *Idomeneo*, but not in the Romantic era. An article as late as 1931 argues that the merit of *Idomeneo* lies in its anticipation of greater things.[12] Hanslick blamed the shortcomings he perceived on the 'insipid and tedious' libretto and the 'stereotyped stage figures', as well as the remoteness of the solo vocal idiom (including the use of high voices) and the deplorably extended recitatives; but he admits that the end of Act II might have been written yesterday. Yet to his surprise the public, respectful during Act I, grew progressively more enthusiastic.

Still less a Wagnerian than Jahn, Hanslick was nevertheless unable to adjust to the dramatic rhythm of an earlier age. His recent experience of Bayreuth may lie behind his indignation at one exception to the generally good stage design: at the end of Act II 'we saw a sort of giant bat (Riesenfledermaus) dancing on the waves, supported, to the general astonishment, by a venerable greyheaded person with a long white beard. This scene needs a real and whole monster, not one scarcely reaching down to its neck.'[13]

The twentieth century

A historically more considered evaluation of *Idomeneo* began with criticism rather than performance. Edward J. Dent devoted two chapters to *Idomeneo* in his pioneering *Mozart's Operas* (1913), more than to *Così fan tutte* and *La clemenza di Tito* combined (of the latter, indeed, Dent had a particularly low opinion).[14] The thoughtful study of Ernst Lert (1921) attributes the style of *Idomeneo* to 'the fever of the Sturm und Drang', but suggests, like Reichardt and Dent, that Mozart had successfully synthesised the diverse influences of Gluck, French opera, and the Neapolitans. Neglecting Mannheim precedents, Lert underlines the experimental nature of *Idomeneo*; and his emphasis on the 'Volk' – the people of Crete – as tragic antagonist to the king is typical of his time.[15]

The propensity to meddle was continued by Ernst Lewicki's two-act version, given in 1917 at Karlsruhe and in 1925 at Dresden; his aim seems to have been the essentially Wagnerian one of bringing Mozart into line with the form and style of Gluck, eliminating, in his own words, 'all characteristic features of the old *opera seria*'.[16] *Idomeneo* was seen as a German *opera manqué*, of uneven quality and antiquated form, its flashes of genius hampered by convention and lacking sustained dramatic vision. This tendency was heavily underlined during the 1931 commemoration (the 175th anniversary of Mozart's birth, and the 150th of *Idomeneo* itself). Most performances that year were still in German.[17] And it was assumed that distortion of a partly Italian-infected original was a duty towards Mozart himself. In accordance with the critical view which reaches from Jahn to Lert, the ensembles and choral music were considered the kernel of the opera's value; the rest was not truly representative of Mozart's Teutonic genius.

By far the most interesting of these versions was for Vienna, by Lothar Wallenstein and Richard Strauss, whose personality is stamped on almost every page; it is considered separately below. For Munich, the opera's original home, Ermanno Wolf-Ferrari likewise recomposed and orchestrated the recitative in collaboration with the theatre dramaturg Ernst Leopold Stahl; the performances were conducted by Hans Knappertsbusch. Despite his Italian origins, Wolf-Ferrari conformed to post-Wagnerian tastes by savage cutting of arias, sparing mainly Ilia's. His recitatives are a weird pot-pourri of Mozart's orchestral motives, taken from scenes otherwise omitted (notably Nos. 22 and 27) and combined with material of his own including, of course, new voice-parts, the result being occasionally reminiscent of Weber.[18] Less extravagant versions were made by Arthur Rother for Dessau and Willy Meckbach for Brunswick. At least the *Neue Zeitschrift für Musik* of Leipzig did not question the propriety of revising Mozart; the reviewer of the Munich production states that after 150 years such revisions were needed to make *Idomeneo* stageworthy.[19] The Dessau critic (following Hanslick) implicitly slighted *Idomeneo* by the description 'Jugendoper' and said it was 'reclaimed for the German stage' despite its dramatic weakness; Rother added little new music (although he orchestrated the recitatives), and Elettra's final aria was revived, but placed *before* the quartet.[20]

Consideration of the letters and the two authentic versions may lead to the conclusion that Mozart never quite finished *Idomeneo*;

but we would not now consider wholesale modernisation, beyond permutation of the authenticated cuts and restorations to suit prevailing conditions, acceptable even in the theatre. But even after the excesses of 1931, the critical tradition was by no means entirely favourable to *Idomeneo*. In his biography of 1935 Eric Blom contradicts Mozart by finding 'lifelessly artificial material, especially in the third act' (he also characteristically derides No. 26 as 'not even good Mendelssohn'). He does not say which arias he finds 'excessively stilted and ornamented', but he appears to deplore foreign influence on Mozart's opera as much as any German.[21] A surprisingly similar view comes from A. A. Abert, who specifies the arias for Raaff as being 'dramatically not at all in keeping with the rest of the work, although at a purely musical level they display complete mastery . . .'[22] It is to be hoped that this attitude, which dismisses the possibility of Raaff's limitations being turned to dramatic use, is now obsolete, for if these pieces of carefully controlled rhetoric are not acceptable there remains little hope for reviving any form of *opera seria*.

The British première of *Idomeneo* was at Glasgow in 1934; there followed performances at Cambridge in 1939 under the tutelage of Dent. The United States and Italy had to wait until 1947. When *Idomeneo* was broadcast in Britain from the 1948 Cambridge Festival, Dent's plea for more stagings uses *Idomeneo* as a stick to attack the moderns, a tactic reminiscent of Reichardt and to a lesser extent Hanslick:

We need 'Idomeneo' . . . to set us a standard: a standard of dignity and nobility for singers, conductors and stage directors, a standard for audiences of intellectual concentration and devotion, a standard too for our own composers of opera, remote enough to remove all danger of direct imitation . . . in the course of the present century we have done a good deal to raise the average standard in musical education and understanding . . . but at the same time we are seriously in danger of losing all sense of the highest standards, those which we have never seen and probably never shall see, standards that can exist only in our imagination. To these – within the limited sphere of opera – 'Idomeneo' might yet point the way.[23]

Idomeneo has since been undertaken by most of the world's principal companies. The equivocal reputation of Mozart's serious operas, however, continued at his birthplace; as recently as the 1949 Salzburg festival *La clemenza di Tito* was amplified by music from *Idomeneo*, including the quartet.[24] Munich revived Wolf-Ferrari in 1955, and Paumgartner produced an amalgam of Munich and Vienna versions for the bicentenary production in Salzburg (1956).

Glyndebourne staged it in 1951, but their centenary recording (1956, under John Pritchard) mauls the recitatives with erratic modulations which, not themselves Mozartian, detract from the force of Mozart's own adventures. Even the 1786 version of 'Fuor del mar' was subjected to cuts.[25]

In recent years *Idomeneo* has received attention from major directors including Jean-Pierre Ponnelle (Cologne, 1971; Zurich, 1980: see Plate 1; New York, 1982), Götz Friedrich (London, Covent Garden, 1978), Trevor Nunn (Glyndebourne, 1983: see Plates 2 and 3), and Frank Corsaro (Los Angeles, 1990: see Plate 4). The score is nowadays presented in an approximately authentic form. Where most modern productions respond less to the musical structure than to the director's desire for post-Wagnerian, or post-verismo, fluidity of action, Trevor Nunn made a virtue of austerity; unlike Ponnelle and Friedrich, for instance, he allowed singers to deliver their arias unhampered by stage movement. His conception was attributed partly to Japanese influence, but he also used motifs which were questioned by Stanley Sadie as 'more Minoan than Classical'.[26]

There has been a gradual tendency to restore the soprano tessitura for Idamante. Contrary to what one might expect, the German performances of 1931 divide into those with a tenor, and those which retain the castrato pitch. Performances of the 1781 version with tenor Idamante are clumsy as well as wrong; these include Schmidt-Isserstedt's 1972 recording,[27] with its eight tenor arias (and only six for soprano). Sung by a tenor, even one so eloquent as Peter Schreier on Karl Böhm's 1979 recording,[28] the role of Idamante fades into insignificance alongside the sturdier music composed for Raaff. An age accustomed not only to Cherubino but to Strauss's Octavian and Composer can appreciate the blend of nobility and vulnerability in Idamante's music, and the youthfulness which makes him almost as attractive a character as Ilia, and his predicament almost as interesting as that of his father. Mozart's Cinna (*Lucio Silla*) and Annio (*Tito*) were intended for female singers, not for a second castrato. A female Idamante is only nominally inauthentic and the best singers, such as Trudeliese Schmidt and Anne Sofie von Otter, have realised the role admirably.[29] Recorded versions show almost equal diversity with the title-role, from the youthful Richard Lewis to the weighty Luciano Pavarotti who, however, both prefer the simpler version of 'Fuor del mar'.[30]

Most modern recordings approach the opera as Mozart is thought to have wanted it performed. Colin Davis's musically

Plate 1 The mask of Neptune. Idomeneo (Werner Hollweg) faces Idamante (Trudeliese Schmidt). Zurich Opera House production (1980), directed and designed by Jean-Pierre Ponnelle. Photo: Susan Schimert-Ramme

Plate 2 The axes of King Minos. Idomeneo (Philip Langridge, centre); with Elettra (Carol Vaness), Ilia (Margaret Marshall), and Idamante (Jerry Handley). Glyndebourne Opera production (1983) by Trevor Nunn, designed by John Napier. Photo: Guy Gravett

Plate 3 Ilia (Margaret Marshall) in a Japanese garden. Glyndebourne Opera production (1983) by Trevor Nunn, designed by John Napier. Photo: Guy Gravett

Plate 4 Ilia (Pamela Coburn) prepares to sacrifice herself. Los Angeles Music
Center Opera production (1990) by Frank Corsaro, designed by Maurice Sendak.
Photo: Frederic Ohringer

inspired 1968 recording is perhaps the last of the old school; nowadays the version used would be regarded as unacceptable (Davis's 1991 recording for Philips implicitly acknowledges this, as well as accepting the female Idamante).[31] The 1973 *NMA* score clarified the textual situation, and Böhm used the true 1786 version. Harnoncourt followed *NMA* for the 1781 version; unfortunately it has since become clear that this represents neither a preferred nor an actual version of Mozart's. Gardiner, in 1991, includes nearly all the 1781 music, some in appendices (such as the recitative which replaces No. 29, and additional versions of the oracle).[32] Besides the loveliest of Ilias, Sylvia McNair, this recording also has the distinction of being the first to use period instruments, with refreshing effect and great beauty of texture.

The performing version by Richard Strauss and Lothar Wallerstein

CHRIS WALTON

> '. . . [eine] grobe Vergewaltigung . . .'
> ('. . . [a] gross act of mutilation . . .')
> Alfred Einstein[33]

For over a hundred years after Mozart's death, *Idomeneo* and *Così fan tutte* all but disappeared from the stage. The latter was consigned by most commentators to the nineteenth-century scrapheap reserved for works immoral and liable to corrupt. The former, ostensibly more wholesome and uplifting, was appraised as an unwieldy, misjudged attempt at an outmoded genre: *opera seria*. *Così*'s return to respectability at the turn of our own century was in no small part thanks to the efforts of Richard Strauss, then a Kapellmeister at the Munich Court Opera. Some thirty years later, Strauss felt moved to render the same service to *Idomeneo*, a work he had long admired – indeed, 'individual numbers such as the 'Zeffiretti' aria and the famous E♭ quartet were favourite pieces of [my] early youth'.[34] The occasion was the 150th anniversary of *Idomeneo*'s first performance in 1781; the instigators of the task were Strauss's protégé Clemens Krauss, conductor and future co-librettist of *Capriccio*, and the producer Lothar Wallerstein, both of whom were active at the Vienna State Opera from the late 1920s.

Whereas Strauss claimed to have made *Così* stageworthy simply by eliminating all extraneous matter with which successive composers and conductors had encumbered Mozart's original score, he judged *Idomeneo* to be in need of more than a mere analogous wash-and-brush-up. For reasons discussed below, he set about adorning *Idomeneo* with additions and revisions of a kind far more radical in approach than those he had so criticised in *Così*. The irony of his inconsistency, however, would seem to have escaped him.

Wallerstein was given the task of translating Varesco's text into German. Rhymed verse was abandoned in favour of prose throughout, and the number-scheme was discarded, leaving merely the division into acts and scenes. The most noteworthy alteration to the libretto was the substitution of Ismene, a priestess of Poseidon, for Varesco's Elettra. Strauss apparently considered one portrayal of Elektra to be sufficient in any man's compositional *œuvre*. Perhaps he saw Mozart's character, with her cries of 'Quando vendetta avrò?' (No. 21), as being too reminiscent of his own creation: 'I think of her as the personification of revenge, and characterised her in music as a goddess of vengeance', said Strauss in 1908.[35] Instead of being a rival for Idamante's love, Ismene/Elektra now becomes a veritable Goebbels in petticoats, jealously guarding the racial purity of her people and determined that her future king should not defile his race by marrying Ilia, a mere Trojan slave.

Strauss's musical amendments can be summarised briefly. He included the new numbers that Mozart had written for the Vienna performance of *Idomeneo* in 1786, but dropped Elettra's aria 'Idol mio' in the second act and those for Idamante ('No, la morte') and Idomeneo ('Torna la pace') in the third. As in some other productions, Arbace lost both his arias and was made a baritone, while the part of the High Priest was assigned to a bass. The tessitura of the other voices was retained, Idamante being given to a female soprano; the 1786 Rondò (K. 490) was removed from the second act to replace 'Non ho colpa' in the first.[36]

The most substantial changes Strauss made were to the 'interminable recitatives',[37] which were heavily cut. Some passages were simply rescored for orchestra (the *semplice* recitative was dropped, and with it the harpsichord), while others were completely rewritten, essentially using musical material from Mozart's score. Strauss himself added two numbers. An orchestral *Interludio* depicting the sea monster's waxing evil influence is placed after the chorus 'Aus Tiefen des Meeres' ('Corriamo, fuggiamo', No. 18). For the closing scene of the opera, Strauss took it upon himself to fulfil Mozart's original intentions (see p. 31, above, and Ex. 6.1) by inserting a quartet for Idamante, Idomeneo, Ilia, and the High Priest before the final chorus 'Eros führt mit mächtigen Waffen ('Scenda Amor'); Strauss dispensed with the ensuing ballet. Both these major additions utilise Mozart's musical material. The middle section of the *Interludio* quotes from the aria 'Torna la pace' that Strauss had dropped, while the ensemble is based upon Idomeneo's recitative 'Popoli, a voi l'ultima legge' (No. 30) and the opening phrase of Ilia's aria 'Wie lang' schon bewein' ich' ('Se il padre perdei'). Nevertheless, the stylistic gap between Mozart and post-*Rosenkavalier* Strauss, apparent at the onset of every recitative, is felt at its strongest in these two interpolations.

The new *Idomeneo* had its première in Vienna on 16 April 1931 (Strauss conducted, with Wallerstein as producer), and received its first performance in Germany several days later, in Magdeburg. The Berlin State Opera waited until November 1932 before staging it. On each occasion the public apparently accorded the work a warm reception but, alas for Strauss, many critics regarded it with a mixture of horror and suspicion. 'Mozart with whipped cream', wrote one critic who was troubled by the stylistic inconsistency and would have preferred less fattening fare.[38] 'It is no advantage that one constantly recognises when it is Mozart's turn to speak and when Strauss's – it is one of the weaknesses of this version' wrote another.[39] Not all the critics were damning – Franz Köppen found words of cautious praise for Wallerstein's 'very skilful' text and the 'responsible' manner in which Strauss had approached his task.[40] But the work's general reception is better represented by Einstein's forthright summary quoted at the head of this chapter. The Strauss–Wallerstein *Idomeneo* was never taken into the repertoire and has not been produced since 1941.

The critics' principal complaint was that the notion of 'authenticity' had been thrown overboard – and yet Strauss would probably have claimed just the opposite. 'Let the critics say what they will. I know my Mozart better than these gentlemen do, and at any rate I love him more ardently than they!' he wrote to Bruno von Niessen.[41] 'Knowledge' and 'Love' of Mozart were the only critical criteria he recognised. Since he firmly believed that he surpassed his contemporaries on both counts, he regarded his aesthetic judgement as infallible: as the foremost German composer, and saviour of *Così*, he could never consider the possibility of his being unfaithful to Mozart's intentions. Oblivious to any potential imbalance in the model–adaptor relationship, he even went so far

Example 6.1

töd - li - che Qual_____ Was ich in schwei - gen - dem

Schmerz___ ge - lit - ten ist nun ver - wan - delt in

Se - lig - keit_____

as to compare his treatment of *Idomeneo* with Wagner's own revision of *Tannhäuser*, which naturally presupposes an abnormally high level of identification with his subject.[42]

The reason Strauss gave for his arrangement of *Idomeneo* was the desire to 'win [it] back for the German stage'.[43] While the 'Germanisation' of the work is an important facet of Strauss's approach, it is much less a political statement than a private act of desperation. Since the turn of the century Strauss had been fêted as the most successful operatic composer since Wagner. He had been director of the German-speaking world's two premier opera houses (Berlin and Vienna), while his dramatic collaborator Hofmannsthal was recognised as the finest living librettist and a major poet in his own right. But by 1929 Strauss had been hounded out of his post in Vienna, his more recent operas were no longer the success that *Rosenkavalier* had been, and – worst of all – Hofmannsthal was dead, having completed only the first act of the libretto for *Arabella*. Strauss can hardly ever have felt a comparable sense of loss of direction.

The timing of the Vienna proposal to revise *Idomeneo* was thus peculiarly lucky, for it provided Strauss with some stability as a temporary alternative to the uncertainty of *Arabella*. Nevertheless, Einstein's word 'Vergewaltigung', with its sexual dimension 'rape', is most appropriate, because Strauss's labour of love for *Idomeneo* constitutes a manifest, often violent act of penetration and possession. In a sense it is an attempt, not to 'win back [*Idomeneo*] for the German stage', but to win back the German stage for himself by uniting his own musical personality with that of Mozart. Perhaps he felt that such a union might prove to the world and to himself that – with or without Hofmannsthal – he was still the one legitimate heir of the German operatic tradition. He might even have considered his revisions justified by an allegorical interpretation of the plot of *Idomeneo*: Idamante/Strauss braving all obstacles before ascending to the throne of his father Idomeneo/Mozart.

The performing version of *Idomeneo* by Strauss and Wallerstein may at first glance appear merely an example of a now *passé* pre-Harnoncourt aesthetic. Yet it no more deserves such criticism than does, say, Stravinsky's treatment of Pergolesi in *Pulcinella* – a work that has more in common with Strauss's *Idomeneo* than the artistic views of their respective creators might lead one to suppose. The musical and dramatic qualities of Strauss's *Idomeneo* cannot be denied; there is also undoubted appeal in its juxtaposition of Mozart, Mozartian pastiche and straightforward late Romanticism. It certainly remained a work of significance for Strauss himself, for he included it in the suggested operatic repertoire for the major German cities in his 'artistic legacy' to Karl Böhm of 27 April 1945.[44] His *Idomeneo* has, nevertheless, slumbered now for fifty years. It will perhaps for ever remain the white elephant of his dramatic *œuvre*; but it is one that should be occasionally allowed out on parade and given the opportunity to blow its own trumpet.

7 *General structure of* Idomeneo

The libretto

For all its allegiance to Franco-Italian reform opera, *Idomeneo* remains within the eighteenth-century norm of alternation of action and introspection, recitative and aria. The three ensembles are more closely merged with the preceding recitative than most of the arias, and all proceed from dialogue to combined voices, yet they function like multi-voiced arias more than the developing ensembles Mozart cultivated in *opera buffa*; they do not further the action. Three static numbers involve solo and chorus, and the full choruses are largely decorative; only the shipwreck, the end of Act II and – static as it is – No. 24 ('O voto tremendo') involve the chorus closely with the principals.

The general structure of the libretto is admirably simple; all three acts begin intimately, and end in public scenes. Act I unfolds the pattern in two stages. A monologue and dialogue are followed by a semi-public scene of rejoicing. The first dramatic event is the announcement of Idomeneo's shipwreck. We are then confronted with the intimate feelings of Elettra, and, after the storm, with those of Idomeneo, before another dialogue. Haltingly, the action returns to soliloquy (Idamante) before the public scene of the divertissement. Such a stop–go process is perhaps a necessary concomitant of exposition. Mozart's cutting axe hardly fell on Act I, which lasts fifty to fifty-five minutes.

The second act, the shortest at around forty-five minutes, begins with an *opera seria* sequence of dialogues and soliloquies before the public scene focuses on Elettra. After the trio the finale brings the elements, the people, and the king into fierce dispute. The libretto does not state when Idamante, Elettra, and even Idomeneo should leave the stage; at the last, our attention is on the chorus and the monster.

95

Act III, much the longest even when 'authentically' cut, begins the most quietly, and builds to a preliminary climax of intimate feelings in the quartet. After the Arbace interlude the scene with the High Priest moves the action toward the Cretan body politic, and the scene shifts to the temple. The struggle at the altar and the oracle itself are as public as the end of Act II. The only doubt is whether 'Madame Elettra' is, in fact, left alone to sing her aria.[1]

This grand design must have been the basis of the original agreed 'plan' to which Leopold Mozart referred (see chapter 5, p.77, n.15). Despite many alterations of detail it remains intact even in the 1786 version, probably prepared without the knowledge of either Leopold or Varesco. The Munich cuts were generally confirmed; the other principal alteration is the removal of a scene between Arbace and Idomeneo (leading to the former's aria, No. 10a). This is only the largest example of Mozart's determination not to waste his musical sweetness on the desert air of explanation. Instead, he provided an opportunity for the second tenor (No. 10b); but the new scene for Ilia and Idamante, which amounts to a mutual declaration of love, deprives their encounter in Act III of any point.

Even if some of his ruthless cutting was dictated by the need to allow time for the ballet, Mozart was certainly justified in protesting that the libretto was too long. It was not Varesco's fault that neither Raaff nor dal Prato could maintain tension during recitatives, although this fact doubtless contributed to the shortening of their dialogue in Act I, and hence to reliance on the *argomento* and printed libretto for the audience's comprehension of what is going on. Reduction of the recitative to a minimum is certainly a step in the Gluckist direction. But the *argomento* does not explain Idomeneo's plan to have Idamante escape from the island, which is outlined in the first scene of Act II; cutting this dialogue (as in the 1786 version) forces the audience to rely on inference. Mozart, however, like Verdi and Berlioz after him, relied on the musical vitality of each scene to overcome such apparent lacunae in the plot.

The four main roles were originally well balanced, although the *primo musico* (dal Prato) and *primo uomo* (Raaff) commanded the greatest exposure (see Table 7.1). Ilia's is the shortest role in the original plan, but it was the only one not seriously affected by the 1781 cuts. Table 7.2 assumes omission of the duet No. 20, the middle of No. 26, and the last three arias, though Idamante's third aria may finally have been included (see chapter 2, p.41, above).

Table 7.1. *Disposition of roles, original version*

	Arias	Ensembles	Other solos	Big orchestral recitatives
Ilia	3	2	None	R. 1
Elettra	3	2	No. 15	R. 4, 29
Idomeneo	3	2	No. 26	R. 12, 18, 27; No. 30
Idamante	3	3	None	R. 7, 27

Table 7.2. *Disposition of roles, 1781 performances*

	Arias	Ensembles	Other solos	Big orchestral recitatives
Ilia	3	1	None	R. 1
Elettra	2	2	No. 15	R. 4, 29
Idomeneo	2	2	None	R. 12, 18, 27; No. 30
Idamante	2 (3)	2	None	R. 7, 27

This version leaves Elettra with five pieces of measured music against four for the others, and her exit after the oracle is very striking even without the aria. It is a minor mystery why the least involved of the four characters acquires such musical prominence; and why in the theatre we do not notice any redundancy, a point which must await later discussion (see chapters 11 and 12, below).

The libretto conventionally marks the division of recitative and measured numbers (aria, ensemble, chorus) by means of versification. Even when simply translating Danchet, Varesco adopted the elevated diction of Metastasio (see chapter 5), who, however, was seldom guilty of Varesco's obscurities.[2] The recitatives predominantly use the traditional lines of seven syllables (*settenarii*) or eleven (*endecasillabi*), with only occasional rhymes.[3] These syllable counts require frequent (but not invariable) elision between adjacent vowels; but at the end of a line, adjacent vowels (as in 'o-ma-i') are counted separately. The punctuation sometimes, though not always, overrides the elision. These points become clear from the first recitative. Hyphens within words indicate divisions necessary for the syllable count; elisions are also conventionally indicated:

1. Quan-d<u>o-a</u>v-ran fi-n<u>e o</u>-ma-i   (7)
2. L'as-pre sven-tu-re m<u>ie</u>? I-l<u>ia-</u> <u>in</u>-fe-li-ce!   (11)
3. Di tem-pe-sta cru-del mi-se-r<u>o a</u>-van-zo,   (11)
4. Del Ge-ni-tor, e de' Ger-ma-ni pri-va   (11)
5. Del bar-ba-ro Ne-mi-co . . .   (7)

In 'omai' (line 1) the first syllable is elided with the previous word, but Mozart correctly sets 'a-i' as two syllables (Ex. 3.2, p.55, above). But in line 2 where the scansion requires 'mie' to be one syllable, Mozart again uses two notes, written as a pitch-repetition but presumably sung with an appoggiatura. He takes advantage of the punctuation to treat it as a line-ending; three beats of expressive string music intervene between 'mie' and 'Ilia'.

All the lines of this recitative are *versi piani*, bearing a principal accent on the penultimate syllable: the setting of 'mie' is typical of a recitative line-ending, a musical convention which arose out of *versi piani*. The first line after the aria, however, is end-accented, a *verso tronco*: 'Ec-co, I-da-man-te, ahi-mè!'. Ostensibly six syllables, such lines stand for a *settenario*; the six-syllable line still has three accents on even-numbered syllables. In setting this line, Mozart elides across the first comma but inserts a rest at the second; he thus requires seven notes. Mozart also treats certain words, such as 'Dio', as two syllables, and 'Idomeneo' as five, even in the middle of a line.[4] In the music, the first twenty-four lines of recitative contain eleven extra 'syllables'. Such anomalies recur throughout, divorcing the musical setting from the already fluid structure of recitative verse. With no disrespect to the latter, therefore, it must be admitted that once set to music it might just as well be prose. Mozart's inattention to its qualities as verse appears also in certain authorised cuts beginning or ending in the middle of a line.

In arias, Varesco mostly followed tradition in using two stanzas of shorter lines, partly rhymed, a procedure susceptible of free repetition and syllable extension without completely destroying the sense. Each stanza consists of *versi piani* until a final *verso tronco*, which enables the voice to cadence on a downbeat. There are normally two rhyming lines within each stanza. In Ilia's third aria (No. 19), written in *ottonari* (eight-syllable lines, with four accents on the odd-numbered syllables), the middle lines are rhymed; the unrhymed line and the *verso tronco* rhyme with their equivalents in the next stanza:

Zeffiretti lusinghieri,	A (*piano*)
Deh volate al mio tesoro:	B (*piano*)
E gli dite, ch'io l'adoro,	B (*piano*)
Che mi serbi il cor fedel.	C (*tronco*)

E voi piante, e fior sinceri,	A
Che ora in affia il pianto amaro,	Bɪ
Dite a lui, che amor più raro	Bɪ
Mai vedeste sotto al Ciel.	C

Varesco rings the changes, for instance offering five-line stanzas of *ottonari* in Idamante's 'Non ho colpa', and three stanzas in Idomeneo's 'Vedrommi intorno'. Chorus texts follow similar patterns, with a preference (certainly agreeing with the composer's) for short lines. But Varesco offers little prosodic variety: the few *versi tronchi* in recitative, and the absence of *versi sdruccioli* (lines of antepenultimate stress), leave an excess of *versi piani*. In the music, however, this matters little.[5] If not greatly imaginative, Varesco's work is competent, and at times (not always thanks to Danchet) poetically uplifting. Nevertheless, it does suggest an author without much experience in viewing his work critically in performing conditions: that input is all Mozart's.

Musical form

Mozart's aria forms are mostly conventional, but their classification is still a matter of controversy. In *Idomeneo* he shows a clear preference for arias which may reasonably be compared to instrumental sonata forms.[6] These fall into two principal classes. The first is binary: two stanzas are each sung twice, in the 'exposition' with a modulation to the dominant (or relative major), and in the reprise which remains in or returns to the tonic. Thus, binary forms end with the second stanza. The second principal class, less well represented in *Idomeneo*, is ternary. The 'exposition' uses the first stanza only, cadencing in the dominant. The second stanza forms a distinct musical unit – a middle section – followed by the reprise of the first stanza, ending in the tonic. The handling of the text to end with the first stanza recalls the by now archaic da capo aria.

In Ilia's second aria, 'Se il padre perdei', Mozart uses the binary design as a framework for particularly rich deployment of a plethora of musical ideas, in the manner of a concertante slow movement. The text has two five-line stanzas of *senarii*, four *versi piani* and one *verso tronco*:

Se il padre perdei	If I have lost my father
La patria, il riposo,	my homeland, my peace,
Tu padre mi sei.	You are a father to me.
Soggiorno amoroso	A sojourn of love
E Creta per me.	Is Crete for me.
Or più non rammento	Now I no longer recall
L'angoscie, gli affanni.	the anguish, the distress.
Or gioia, e contento,	Now joy and happiness,
Compenso a miei danni	consolation for my injuries,
Il ciel mi diè.	Heaven grants me.

The five-line stanzas are grammatically subdivided, the first as three plus two lines, which Mozart marks by perfect cadences (bars 26, 69) corresponding to the full stops.[7] Imperfect cadences (bars 39, 81) divide the second stanza into two plus three lines. In each case the main cadence is followed by new, sharply characterised thematic material. The first clear punctuation introduces the dominant key (bar 27) with the first phrase given unaccompanied to the quartet of solo wind instruments (Ex. 7.1b; Ex. 7.1a shows the opening).

In the second stanza Ilia denies that her memories are bitter; the music (Ex. 7.1c) perhaps questions her denial. But after a half-close on the dominant of the dominant (bar 39), further new material (Ex. 7.1d) characterises 'Gioia e contento', and the last line includes an elaborate measured cadenza (Ex. 7.1e) in which the voice and wind flourish in turns. The strings provide their own cadence (Ex. 7.1f). The two-bar link by the solo wind restores the tonic E♭, settled by a string cadence (upbeat to bar 58) which delicately elides with the return of the first stanza, text and music. The reprise corresponds in length to the exposition. 'B' begins in the subdominant and it returns to the tonic (bar 70), which is unchallenged by 'C' (bar 84), 'E' (bar 90), or 'F' (bar 106). The exact repeat of what was previously a link, followed by the string cadence (bars 108–11 repeat bars 55–8) is the very picture of contentment.[8]

Overall symmetry is most elegant when details are asymmetrical. In the reprise 'A' is unchanged and 'B' rearranged within an equivalent length, seven bars. 'C', however, is extended by repetition; and the voice part is reconceived so that its tessitura corresponds to the exposition despite the new harmonic situation. The setting of 'Or più non rammento' is equally affecting in the reprise. The bass line is transposed, the voice adjusted: in the exposition it centres on the descent from f"–c", in the reprise, while rising a little higher, it is focused on a lower pitch, the dominant (b♭'). The rising sixth of the exposition is answered by a chain of falling sevenths in the reprise (Ex. 7. 1g). Even where a mechanical repetition was available to him, Mozart heightens the expression: 'E' is rearranged so that the voice can rise to b♭" (Ex. 7. 1h).[9]

This aria design is also used for Nos. 1 ('Padre, germani': see chapter 8), 4 ('Tutto nel cor vi sento': see chapter 11), 7 ('Il padre adorato'), and 13 ('Idol mio'). Mozart uses a variant of this form with the same disposition of stanzas, but where the second half does not return at once to the tonic and the opening music. Instead a procedure used in sonatas by D. Scarlatti and J. C. Bach is adopted: in the reprise the first stanza is tonally unstable, and only the second corresponds to the exposition, though now in the tonic. This form is used in the quartet and No. 29 ('D'Oreste, d'Aiace'), pieces of exacerbated emotion: the recapitulated second group in No. 29 emphasises the minor tonic, and the quartet subjects its material to exceptional harmonic and polyphonic intensification.[10]

In ternary sonata-arias only the first quatrain is recapitulated, but principles of symmetry and partial asymmetry continue to apply. In 'Zeffiretti lusinghieri' nothing in the form of the poetry (see above) prevented Mozart from using binary form. Instead, at the point where the second stanza would appear in a binary aria, the first is repeated in the dominant with a new melodic idea. This expansive three-section design is suited to a peaceful soliloquy, and Mozart presumably wanted the mood of the first quatrain to precede Idamante's unexpected entry.

The tonal and melodic aspects of both settings of the first quatrain (forming the first and third sections of the aria) are related to each other in exactly the same way as the two halves of 'Se il padre perdei'. The exposition ends with a greatly expanded cadence featuring a prolonged f♯" on 'fedel'. The reprise begins like the exposition, as far as the imperfect cadence on 'tesoro' (bars 29 and 93). There is no short cut; the quatrain is repeated in the tonic, the voice part skilfully rearranged to preserve the tessitura of the second part of the exposition (Ex. 7.2). The prolonged high note is now only an e", but it rises chromatically to f♯" (bar 129) for a still more emphatic cadence. In a coda typical of sonata thinking, Mozart brings back the original melody of the second stanza, otherwise missing from the reprise (bars 38, 125).

Example 7.1

f

violins

violas

g

Or più non ram - men - to l'an - go - scie, gli af -

flute oboe

fan - ni, gli af - fan - - - ni,

horn, bassoon

h **H** 90

diè, or gio - - - - - -

bassoon

horn

oboe

flute

ia e con - - ten - -

to il cie - lo mi diè.

For the second quatrain Mozart could either continue in the same tempo and metre, or choose new ones. In No. 19 the middle section makes use of music from the exposition (the orchestral scales, bars 66 and 68), a clear analogy with a sonata development section.[11] But No. 12 ('Fuor del mar') is of the same general type as 'Zeffiretti lusinghieri'; any archaism lies in its style, not its form. No. 31 ('Torna la pace') retains the sonata-like relation between the first and third sections, but uses a contrasting tempo, whereas the only other aria with a contrasting middle section, No. 27 ('No, la morte io non pavento'), has outer sections related like the two

Example 7.2

No. 19

parts of No. 29: the reprise starts with a version of the opening motive on dominant harmony, so the two new settings of the quatrain are different in detail from the exposition.

Mozart surely selected aria designs and manipulated their details with a view to characterisation, which he conceived in the light of the singers available to him. Where Arbace's arias are deliberately stiff, the ternary 'Zeffiretti lusinghieri' has a modern, developmental middle section. Ilia's other arias are richly expressive binary designs, as are Elettra's most characteristic utterances. Elettra's 'Idol mio' follows the binary plan with artless simplicity (reinforced by strings-only orchestration), contriving to be idyllic without altering one's conception of the character. Idamante's forms are always clear, perhaps reflecting dal Prato's simplicity but also emblematic of straightforward nobility; for which reason the elaborate rondò with obbligato violin (No. 10b) seems to fall outside appropriate stylistic bounds.[12]

Mozart uses a modern three-part form (if an archaic style) for the active 'Fuor del mar', an old-fashioned design for Idomeneo's abdication ('Torna la pace'). A less conventional form is used in No. 6, 'Vedrommi intorno'. The slow opening exhausts two quintains of text, the first leading towards the dominant, the second ('Nel sen trafitto', from bar 27) actually in it. At this point a return to the opening would be possible, making a simple binary aria. Instead, the tempo changes to allegro with a new quintain ('Qual spavento'); there is no reprise. The allegro resolves the dominant modulation by close adherence to the tonic, albeit often the tonic minor. After three sonata-type arias this openness of form is an effective metaphor of Idomeneo's confusion.[13] The only other two-tempo numbers on this pattern are the equally distressed trio in Act II (No. 16), and the rapturous 1781 love duet (No. 20a), which conforms to a well-established duet pattern.[14] In 1786, Mozart reduced the duet to a single movement (No. 20b), closer in length to an *opera buffa* duet, but retained a hold on his 1781 conception by use of the same material.

For choruses, Mozart felt able to respond to the dramatic situation directly. The binary form of the shipwreck chorus (No. 5) is a minimum gesture towards formality, and at the end of Act II the chorus's contributions are still more naturalistic. On the other hand, the move to ritual (after the revelation in No. 23) brings appropriately symmetrical forms (Nos. 24 and 26, separated by a march). The presence of a march in each act marks the usefulness to a dramatic composer of the most conventional rhythmic patterns, and also shows Mozart's care in tailoring his conventional material to each situation. No. 8, the march for the disembarkation, is suitably festive. The other marches both cover scene-changes: No. 14, scored for wind, is an outdoor piece, whereas No. 25 breathes an air of mystery which anticipates another temple, in *Die Zauberflöte*. The choral sections in the divertissements, like the dances of which, indeed, they sometimes form a part, have a suitable lucidity. Their firm structures, indeed, underline the boldness of ending Act II with a divertissement-substitute (No. 18, 'Corriamo, fuggiamo') of frightening realism. But such modulation from the intimate to the public and from formal, even ceremonial forms of interaction to raw feeling, is characteristic of the whole opera and forms its boldest departure from decorum.

8 Two soliloquies

Ilia's opening recitative and aria

The recitative 'Quando avran fine omai' and aria 'Padre, germani' fall into a conventional pattern for soliloquy: the orchestrated recitative explores Ilia's situation and conflicting emotions, while the aria is their summation and, importantly, an occasion for the singer to do more than declaim. But we should not simplistically regard the recitative as the domain of the dramatist, and the aria as that of the singer. Mozart takes the role of dramatist without compromising the service he offers to both librettist and performer.

Few recitative-aria pairs are so carefully planned as this. At the end of the overture (Ex. 1.4) D major is coloured by a morose inflection which suggests G minor, widely regarded as Mozart's favourite key of pathos.[1] Ilia herself completes the move to G minor, enhanced by a false relation (her f♮"; bass f♯). The main tonal area is prolonged by a move towards the subdominant; a threefold motivic statement (from bar 12) brings back G minor (bar 19). Then a sustained texture suggests modulation to F, but is cancelled by two diminished sevenths, an essentially arbitrary procedure which restores G minor for the next motivic intervention (Andante *agitato*, bar 27; Ex. 8.1).

This pattern of departure and return governs the whole recitative. As it proceeds, we learn the basic facts of the dramatic argument, and how they appear to Ilia. Narrative sections use *semplice* recitative; emphatic expressions of feeling, often represented in the libretto by no more than disconnected exclamations, require the orchestra. After arrival in B♭ (bars 29–32) a moving Adagio dilates upon E♭ harmony (bars 34–40). At this point the recitative could have ended, or led to an aria, perhaps in E♭: but the thought of Elettra intervenes. The subsequent semplice passage reaches B minor (bar 50); however, the cadence is interrupted, bringing G major

Example 8.1

for the final obbligato section until a minor subdominant (bar 64) leads to the close in G minor.

Recitatives are often required to form a coherent bridge between numbers in widely divergent keys (such as No. 20 in A; No. 21 in E♭). Here we sense an obsession, symbolised by the recurrence of G minor, which is retained for the aria; almost inevitably some pitch-configurations also connect them (Ex. 8.2 shows only the more obvious ones). The closure of the recitative into the first bars of the aria (Ex. 3.3a) marks the channelling of Ilia's problems into the emotional therapy of measured music.

The recitative's motivic invention responds freely to Ilia's moods. Her initial preoccupation with sorrow brings a gentle rising figure over a falling bass; uncertain, yet not without ardour. After 'Ilia infelice!' (bar 4) the first violins curve around g″ and descend, while the seconds mirror them, a textural feature which recurs in the sacrifice scene. As Ilia recalls her rescue by Idamante, strings underline her question (bar 11): for what dire fate has she been spared? The brusque threefold Allegro melts at bars 20–21 into a dominant seventh on C (bar 21) as tender thoughts of Idamante

Example 8.2

overtake thoughts of vengeance. The failure of this dominant seventh
to resolve is an analogue of her ambivalent feelings. When G minor
is uncertainly restored (bar 27), violent syncopation, huge violin
intervals, and tremolo reflect the turmoil of gratitude, hate, and love.

Unusually within a recitative, the Adagio in E♭ forms a closed
musical statement. A harmonic antecedent (bars 34–7) reaches a
restful cadence-figure (motive F); after Ilia's climactic g♭" (bar 38),
a lyrical cadence functions as harmonic consequent. The exclamations of the text are sensitively contradicted by this musical
completeness, conveying the decision of which she is as yet
unconscious: love will prevail. When she thinks of Elettra, the
suggestively biting figure, syncopated and chromatic (bars 40–3),
rises a tritone, E♭ to A; it recurs at the retransition in the aria
(bars 56–8, violins: see Ex. 8.2), where, however, it can hardly
refer to Elettra. On both appearances it is counterpointed with the
'tragic' diminished fourth of 'Ilia infelice' (recitative, second violins,

bars 40–3). The last recitative motive, in G major, consists of a powerful ascent negated by the response in the bass. The musical imagery anticipates the High Priest in Act III, perhaps because (prophetically) Ilia refers to her metaphorical executioners: revenge, jealousy, hate, and love. Syncopation, swift scales, and dotted rhythms mark this as a passage of 'Sturm und Drang'. Exceptionally within a recitative, some words ('sbranate si') are repeated; the second 'si', an Adagio minim on f♯", is the longest note since the same pitch, notated g♭", in bar 38 (see Ex. 3.3a, p. 57).

By this richly inventive recitative, linked with both overture and aria, Mozart set a standard of tonal coherence and continuity which in the event he did not maintain. He had no systematic policy of breaking down the boundaries which conventionally separate recitative from aria. Here formal elision marks the extremes and the centre of the aria. The five-bar introduction establishes its resigned mood while acting as the cadence of the recitative, and the final tonic lasts only a quaver, whereupon a brief orchestral surge, its bass using the 'tragic' motive of 'Ilia infelice', initiates the next recitative. In the centre, the second stanza cadences in the secondary key area (B♭, bar 56), and the first returns after only one bar; but the original melody is only recovered two bars later (Ex. 8.3). This formal device packs the sensation of a development section into three bars of retransition, a moment of extreme harmonic tension enhanced by the dynamics (*sfp* on every second quaver: all previous similar markings – bars 9, 12, 23, etc. – have been on strong beats).

In the first stanza, the third and fourth lines of text proceed immediately to the relative major with a completely new texture. Eventually Ilia's mixed feelings emerge in lyricism: Crete, now her 'cagion' (prison), will soon be her 'soggiorno amoroso' (No. 11). The second stanza is all in B♭. It is linked to the first by violin syncopation; the melody, hitherto exclamatory (except for 'cagion tu sei'), takes on a smoother and more ornate character, in a texture of equal counterpoint between outer parts (Ex. 8.4a). The bass motive has recently been heard (at the end of the overture), but, resolving upwards in a B♭ arpeggio, this version of 'motive C' is gentle, even ingratiating. If it is Idamante's motive, it could suggest that Ilia has already lost her struggle against love: 'ungrateful to my blood, I cannot hate him'. Repetition, customary at this point in an aria, underlines the point, as does the warm background of sustained woodwind (bar 41). The repeat is extended by a far from anguished, even affectionate, cadential postponement (bars 52–5).

Example 8.3

Example 8.4a

Example 8.4b

After its ambiguous start (Ex. 8.3), the reprise is exact until the 'Grecia' motive (originally a stark unison, bar 14) is clothed in a fiercely rising tremolando (bar 66). Ilia's weakening resolve and growing misery appear in her failure to match the minim rhythm of the wind instruments; the phrase 'Cagion tu sei' (bar 73) lacks its earlier lyricism (compare bar 17), and the lively three-note motive used in bars 23–7 is replaced by undifferentiated tremolo, the altered melody soaring to a pained top A.

Example 8.5

The recapitulation of the second stanza is more exact, as sonata form demands, but Mozart skilfully remoulds the voice part over a replica of the earlier accompaniment. Where simple transposition would produce e♭, high g″ is still placed on the first beat of the bar, but 'quel' is again g″; transposition would produce b♭″, perhaps not ideal for Wendling (Ex. 8.4b). The repeat of this passage is followed by an extended cadence, with another g″ (and *sfp*), where previously there has been f″; and the gracious B♭ cadence (bars 53–5) is transformed into a fervently chromatic complaint (Ex. 8.5, bars 108–11). Despite the repetition of the two stanzas, the moods of the second part do not duplicate the first. Instead, the conventional form of the aria conveys a dramatic point: Ilia recognises her weakness, but she cannot yet be reconciled to it. Accordingly Idamante finds her ready to listen, but not to accept his avowal.

The centrepiece: 'Fuor del mar'

Idomeneo's recitative (R. 12) links two arias of contrasting sentiment and tonality; indeed, the recitative is more strongly connected to the previous aria than to No. 12. Idomeneo has just listened to 'Se il padre perdei' and is disturbed by Ilia's 'equivocal' speech: the recitative opens with a distorted form, on still-muted strings, of the obbligato wind phrase (Ex. 7.1b). Why is Crete 'a home of love' for the orphaned princess? Her joy is untimely. The cadence of the aria returns, still in E♭, followed by a brief chromatic surge to a diminished seventh; he understands that she loves Idamante. The mutes are whipped off. A pointed figure marks an enharmonic modulation towards F♯ minor, and a variant of Ilia's 'Gioia e contento' ironically frames his declaration: 'I am not deceived; their love is mutual.' This moment of recognition coincides with the arrival of D major, the key of the aria. As the king realises that Neptune will have three victims, the rich harmonic accretions of a minor cadence cast a tragic shadow.[2] The first quatrain of the aria brings images of menace:

Fuor del mar, ho un mar in seno	Free of the sea, I have a sea in my breast
Che del primo è più funesto,	More deadly than the first,
E Nettuno ancor in questo	And Neptune again in this one
Mai non cessa minacciar.	Never ceases to threaten.

Unlike most arias in *Idomeneo*, 'Fuor del mar' has a formal ritornello, strongly affirmative after the recitative's B minor cadence: even the brass contribute to the arpeggio melody. If this refers to the opening of the overture (by inversion), there is no chromatic challenge to the authority which resides in this powerful descending figure, unless it is the C♮ of bar 4, quickly neutralised in a baroque-style tutti (bar 7). Richness of texture rather than uncertainty of mood is implied in the contrapuntal passage from bar 9.

The ritornello is assertive, but this firmly structured ternary aria, nevertheless, contains signs of human weakness. The singer returns to the opening d', rather than matching the decisive orchestral descent (Ex. 8.6). C♮ then features in a descent to the subdominant G, recalling his previous aria, although 'Vedrommi intorno' extends this subdominant leaning much further.[3] Then the neutralising C♯ falls despite being a leading-note (bar 21); and until bar 25 the voice mostly presents falling shapes. Does this aspect, not present in the ritornello, signify Idomeneo's weakness?[4]

Example 8.6

Yet, despite such equivocal details, the music of the first two lines taken as a whole retains the assertive character of the ritornello. The voice achieves a firm D major cadence (bars 31–2); thus this musical period is an expanded version of the basic shape in the first line, eluding the lower tonic and, after asserting E by way of D♯, rising to g' before the cadence (Ex. 8.7).

The next two lines begin with brusque half-bar imitations (from bar 33), and constitute the modulation, arrival in the dominant

Example 8.7

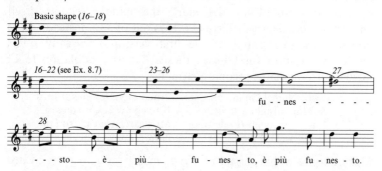

region being signalled by the first sustained f$\sharp$' (bar 39). The two versions of the aria diverge here, the dominant cadence being at bar 51 in the original version, bar 46 in the revision (bar numbers henceforth are in the form original/revised). As the last two lines are repeated, the fall to e', ending the first coloratura flourish (47/–), is reproduced in diminution at the section's cadence (72–4/57–9: Ex. 8.8).

Example 8.8

The voice's g$\sharp$ (57/52) brings a sinister sonority, three bars of diminished seventh animated by syncopation and a gurgling semiquaver figure tossed from violas and basses to the woodwind. As they take on a life of their own, the semiquavers increasingly suggest the capricious movements of the sea, and recall earlier intimations of a storm. The illustration of menace ('minacciar') brings further coloratura, imitating these semiquavers (61/–), and syncopation (64/56). The revised version (the two join in 73/57) has an equally strong dominant cadence, and the central ritornello (76/60), reminiscent of a concerto, restores the vigour of the opening.

In the dedication of *Alceste*, Gluck reproached composers for rushing through the second stanza of a ternary aria, even where the text implies that it should be particularly expressive. In the revised form of 'Fuor del mar', the middle section, itself unchanged, bulks large (thirty-two bars out of 152, instead of 174 in the 1781 form); but in the first version it already offers impressive support for Gluck's thesis. A curt modulation to F♮ (82/66) introduces the second quatrain:

Fiero Nume! Dimmi almeno:	Proud God: tell me at least
Se al naufragio è si vicino	If to shipwreck is so close
Il mio cor, qual rio destino	My heart, what harsh fate
Or gli vieta il naufragar?	Now prevents that shipwreck?

Mozart begins with a variant of 'Ho un mar in seno' (bar 17), treated imitatively and traversing an immense tonal space (Table 8.1).

Table 8.1

	84/68	89/73	93/77	94/78	95/79	99/83
[A]	F		V of B♭ → evaded	V of A →	A mi. cadence evaded →	F♯ mi. sequence cadence

This chilling image of desolation is achieved by moving a semitone down between dominants (92–4/76–8, from B♭ to A) and then down a minor third: A minor is linked to F♯ minor by reinterpreting a single diminished seventh (98/82), before Mozart restores order by associating these keys in a sequence which uses a rhythm virtually absent from the first section (Ex. 8.9).

In the reprise, Mozart shows characteristic finesse in reworking the modulatory passage ('E Nettuno . . .'). He begins on the subdominant and moves to the home dominant (133/117) by a sturdy, even menacing, sequence. The coloratura (first version) comes earlier, leaving space for an improvised cadenza (which, however, is marked for omission in the Munich performing material). Massive symmetry (so different from the insecure design of 'Vedrommi intorno') does not preclude a return of the menacing semiquavers (the three-bar diminished seventh, 153/131), but it also implies the recovery of the principal topic, reinforced by a final ritornello and emphatic cadence.[5]

Designed as a showpiece for Raaff, 'Fuor del mar' is also, or perhaps therefore, the dramatic centrepiece of the opera. It is one of the most fully instrumented pieces, the first aria with trumpets, and in the 'main key', D major.[6] Yet it may be understood in more than one way, and its impact depends more than that of Ilia's arias

Example 8.9

on the actual performance. Its vehemence is enhance the coloratura obligatory in a grand aria for Raaff; the revised version is decidedly weaker in impact, for Mozart used display to suggest a surge of energy. The weary Idomeneo of the sea-shore and the scene with Arbace now shows his kingly stature. The aria implies defiance; at the end of Act II, coincidentally or not in the same key, Idomeneo openly challenges the gods. Arguably, therefore (but see chapter 10 below), the aria represents the identification of the king with the principal tonality of the opera, one of those most readily recognisable in eighteenth-century music, and here associated by an opening arpeggio and instrumentation with the overture.

But *should* an aria concerned with divine menace, shipwreck, and death, be so confidently formed an assertion of the 'tonic'? And why, when the second stanza points ahead to the king's defiance, does Mozart adopt a ternary form, ending with the first stanza? The lively rhythms support the harmony and form; even the desolate middle section is governed by a gavotte-like metre, while the overall 'topic' of the aria is a march.[7] A stereotyped view of the expressive capacities of major and minor might lead a post-Romantic listener, or even one well acquainted with Gluck, to expect the minor mode in an aria of defiance.

But we ought not to assume a simple correlation between music and words, least of all in a dramatic work. The brilliance of D major reminds us that tragedy includes illumination. The modulatory direction of the recitative suggests that here at least D major symbolises Idomeneo's understanding and acceptance of the full horror of his situation. The major mode implies more resolution than the minor; both senses of 'resolution' are appropriate as a counterpoint to the literal meaning of the words. Resolution, too, is implicit in the structure. Idomeneo understands the full extent of the tragedy which, paradoxically, his own salvation may bring about; he cannot see a solution, but he finally faces the problem from which, in Act I, he literally ran away. After the yielding and agitated 'Vedrommi intorno', this aria demonstrates his full stature and makes him worthy of sympathy when he is no longer able to conceal the need for Idamante's sacrifice.

9 *The musical language of* Idomeneo

A serious opera composer, even one as fluent as Mozart, is absorbed in this work over a relatively extended period. It is natural, therefore, that singularities of style should contribute to its particular character, what in the nineteenth century would have been called its 'colorito' or 'tinta'.[1] Musical ideas are prone to recur in an intriguing fashion, although not necessarily in circumstances which impel one to search for what Dent called a 'ridiculous' or 'Wagnerian' name.[2] This chapter seeks to describe aspects of the musical language which have struck responsive chords in one listener's extended exposure to *Idomeneo*.

It is no part of my intention to demonstrate that the opera is musically an 'organic whole'. It may be that, of course, but only if conceived as an inextricable combination of a dramatic idea, words, scenery, and music. The music is undoubtedly the most important single element, but it is never independent of the others. Mozart himself, in excising so much as the performances approached, made it clear that musical integrity was not the principal criterion in shaping his work.

In practice external factors, apparently restraints upon the composer's fantasy, may contribute positively to the unique colour of an opera. In *Idomeneo* one such factor was the personnel of Munich (see chapter 3, above), because of whom the orchestration is of unparalleled richness; Mozart had to order trumpet mutes from Salzburg, but Munich provided the four horns, the excellent strings, and wind players clearly equal to the Viennese for whom he composed later. But orchestral players do not impose a style to the extent that singers may. That singers' idiosyncrasies affected Mozart is clear from the correspondence relating to *Die Entführung* ('I wrote it expressly to suit Adamberger's voice . . . ' and 'I have sacrificed Constanze's aria a little to the flexible throat of Mlle Cavalieri': letter of 26 September 1781). Mozart worked just

as closely with the Munich cast. Was it a trait of Dorothea
Wendling that led to the virtual echo of her second aria during her
third? The context is very different, the falling seventh unmistakably
the same; compare Ex. 7.1g with Ex. 9.1.

Example 9.1

The proclivities and limitations of Raaff unquestionably affect the
role of Idomeneo, perhaps suggesting the leaning to the subdominant
by way of a flattened seventh which begins both 'Vedrommi
intorno' and 'Fuor del mar'. Was it Elisabeth Wendling's expertise
in totally different styles which allowed Mozart the potent characterisation inherent in the contrast between 'Tutto nel cor' and
'Idol mio'? As for dal Prato, did he have a predilection for the key
of B♭? Mozart may have begun each scene in which he appears
(until the last) in that key not to symbolise the prince, still less to
provide some kind of structural network of tonalities (on which
see chapter 10, below), but simply to help an unsteady performer.
Certainly it took him considerable compositional effort, at least in
Act III, where Idamante's entrance follows soon after an aria at
the opposite tonal pole, No. 19 (in E). But however mundane their
cause, such gestures may have quite a startling effect.[3]

Any work based on a common-practice style – which is to say
any work of Mozart not written purely for private delectation –
will obtain effects from elements of that practice; this is particularly
true in harmony, where the predominant phraseology and triadic
language permits controlled use of dissonant and chromatic structures. There is no need to particularise the fundamental harmonic
language of *Idomeneo*. But just as Mozart took instrumentation to
an extreme, so he challenged the harmonic limitations which most
of his contemporaries observed, and most listeners welcomed. His
richness of harmony partly results from a concentration of chromatic
elements which are conventional in themselves, and it may most
easily be observed, free of the constraints imposed by periodic
rhythm, in the recitatives.[4]

Mozart composed the simple recitative at top speed, and necessarily relied on melodic and harmonic clichés as the singers had to
learn them in a short time. Yet he included progressions which are

quite startling, given that only a keyboard was available to realise them. The first dialogue (R. 2) shows subtle, almost hidden repetition of a three-note bass descent, and already engages to an exceptional degree in deceptive resolution. In Idamante's opening speech, the second and fourth bass-notes imply chords with a dominant function ('V' in Ex. 9.2). As he addresses his followers, the descent prolongs B♭ through its subdominant; the speech ends with the expectation of a cadence (bar 3 in Ex. 9.2a). But a bass E

Example 9.2

replaces the expected B♭; it is not figured, but by long convention it stands for a first inversion of C. This progression is a cliché designed to make a dramatic point – Idamante turns to address Ilia – and is resolved back to F (bar 5). As he tells Ilia that the Argive fleet has been sighted, a second bass descent begins a quiet move to the dominant of C (bar 12). So far, therefore, the larger pattern is of equable rises by a fifth (B♭, F, C).

Ilia's reply brings another tragic diminished fourth (motive G, bar 13; compare Ex. 1.6, which was heard seven bars before Ex. 9.2). Here (Ex. 9.2b) the final D♯ supports a B major first inversion, giving sharpness (literal and metaphorical) to her reply, marked in the libretto 'with irony'. The chord is modified, with Mozart's first bass figuring, to a bitter diminished seventh, before resolving to E, again a tritone away from the framing key of the recitative (bar 16). In Idamante's response Mozart makes discreet use of harmonic surprise to underline a psychological point. At 'più non dolerti' ('Grieve no more') the third three-note bass descent reaches C. C major would naturally follow E minor, but it is replaced by the markedly more distant C minor (bar 18). By replicating the three-note descent Mozart reaches A♭ ('generoso', bar 21); the bass has now used five notes of the whole-tone scale ('W' in Ex. 9.2b). Idamante's mind is ahead of his speech; he is preparing to confess that he himself remains imprisoned by her beauty, which brings a raw inversion of the diminished fourth, A♭ rising to E♮.

The continuation surrounds a bass G with almost every chromatic permutation of adjacent pitches, including juxtaposed dominants on G (root position, bar 32) and G♭ (third inversion, bar 33).[5] This desolate sound reflects the picture Ilia evokes: Troy's proud walls are reduced to the level of the vast plain, and she owes a duty of unending tears. The immediate progression is towards F as dominant of B♭ minor (bar 35). B♭ may be the tonic of the whole scene, but more significantly here it is a tone below what was predictable a moment before.

Sinking a tone, symbolic of disturbance or depression, is a special feature of *Idomeneo*. Its impact is devastating in Elettra's first recitative and aria (see chapter 11, below) and the chorus No. 17 ('Qual nuovo terrore') where B♭ minor overwhelms the C minor which the context would lead one to predict (bar 32). It affects Idamante's second aria (bar 23, C minor follows D minor) and appears when he is again rejected by his father; in the Quartet it reproduces itself to reach a third key (C minor, B♭ minor, A♭ minor, bars 80–5). This type of progression attains its apotheosis in the sacrifice scene, when Ilia challenges the Priest to take her as victim instead of Idamante (Ex. 9.3).

Example 9.3

The first bass intervals include a tritone and diminished fourth, governed by a characteristic intensifying progression up a fifth, A to E; the subsequent F♯ dominant seventh suggests a further ascent to B. Instead the bass continues to descend chromatically. There are conventional ways of harmonising such a descent, which is affective in itself; Mozart prefers a sequence of dominant seventh and unrelated minor triads in first inversion. The best explanation for this progression is that each note of the F♯ chord moves a semitone (F♯–F♮; A♯–A♮; C♯–D). This kind of criterion, however, is only routinely required in analysis of later music, beyond Wagner's *Tristan.* Mozart emphasises the disruption by repeating the progression, dominant sevenths on E and D 'resolving' to C and B♭ minor, before clearing the air by arrival on C (bar 112). There are thus four dominant sevenths separated by whole-tone steps, and a similarly descending sequence of minor triads.

Such sequences could in theory be indefinitely extended. Mozart rights the balance with the most solid of recitative progressions, descending fifths (C–f–B♭), obviously heading for E♭ in bar 115.[6] This might reassure his audience, but the explanation for a change of process in recitative nearly always lies in the text. Ilia has proclaimed Idamante's innocence; as Idomeneo's son he is the hope of the kingdom. With desperation, over the shifting sands of enharmony, she insists that they have misinterpreted the divine will; heaven wants the blood of Greece's enemies, not her sons. She is innocent, and now their friend, but 'I am Priam's daughter' (bar 112), her very name the enemy of Greece. Ilia's reasoning is grandly specious, but her speech is invested by the music with the power and desperation of self-sacrificing love; whereupon the earth trembles and the oracle proclaims the mercy of Neptune.

The harmonic originality of *Idomeneo* is not confined to scenes of emotional turbulence, and it may be linked with another significant feature, the recurrence of short but pointed musical images in separate musical numbers. The texture of *Idomeneo*, more than most music of the time, is filled with the richest harmonic flavours of the period such as diminished sevenths and augmented sixths. Some of these are discussed in chapter 11 as part of the 'Elettra plot', but their role extends more widely. The scarcely less ambiguous 'half-diminished' seventh is less common in the eighteenth century, although easily construed as implying a dominant major ninth. It enters *Idomeneo* as a honeyed woodwind chord in No. 15 ('Placido è il mar', bars 17 and 63), and returns, soon enough for memory to link the two events, in the Trio (bar 100, at 'clemenza'). Both chords ('T' in Ex. 9.4) are followed by simple cadences with identical bass. The text thus singled out in the Trio represents the last residue of the hope embodied in No. 15. Further half-diminished sevenths appear in the duet (No. 20a, bar 96), Arbace's aria No. 22 (bar 40), and, warmly sustaining the heroism of Idamante, in the sacrifice scene (bar 76), just before the aria 'No, la morte'.

On one level a conventional expression of typical *opera seria* form, the Trio (No. 16) is shot through with dramatic irony, reflected in a motivic content which relates to the overture in several places. None of the characters apparently believes in the journey for which they implore heaven's clemency (even Elettra sounds doubtful; perhaps she hears Idamante's despairing 'O Ilia!'). At bar 36 the strings play a distant relative of motive C and at the approach to the Allegro the rising scales suggest the end of the overture. Near the start of the Allegro (bar 67), a sturdy arpeggio filled by glissandi recalls the majesty of the overture (motive A) and anticipates more exactly the speech of the High Priest.

It is not easy to assess facts such as these, which tend to flock to one's attention without proclaiming their significance, as would a true leitmotif. But it is surely striking that motives A and C should all recur in the next set piece, No. 18 ('Corriamo, fuggiamo'), with

Example 9.4

motive E at the very end, as in the overture (see Ex. 1.8). A (chorus, bars 5–6) is without glissandi, and the more accurate version of 'C' (bars 26–7) is virtually inaudible (bars 7–10 are related to motive C and also to Elettra's aria, No. 4). This piece in D minor parallels the D major overture; and here the king's fortunes are at their nadir. A fatalistic inversion of motive A opens the great Quartet. But arpeggios are the commonest material of tonal music; and it would paradoxically be superficial to seek out all the many possible references to this general idea and try to burden them with some exact significance.[7] A dramatic context suggestive of authority will tend to elicit a relatively limited range of responses from any eighteenth-century composer, and motive A may have no more than an immediate affective significance, in the Trio and in No. 23, when the authority specifically resides in the High Priest.

The rhythmic language of music is perhaps its most immediate passport to a listener's understanding of fundamental topics, although in music of this period rhythmic activity is nearly always coordinated with harmony and phrasing.[8] In the late eighteenth century solemnity is mainly associated with duple time, while the principal dance metres are triple. The first use of $\frac{3}{4}$ in *Idomeneo* is the chorus of rejoicing, No. 3; at this tempo, $\frac{3}{4}$ does not recur until the entr'acte (Ciaconna). In the dramatic scenes of Act I, only the slow section of 'Vedrommi intorno' (No. 6) is in $\frac{3}{4}$; and in Act II, only the slow section of the Trio. The rest of Act II is in $\frac{2}{4}$ and $\frac{4}{4}$, with two exceptions. No. 15 ('Placido è il mar') is the first piece in compound time ($\frac{6}{8}$); this contributes as much as its tonality and instrumentation to the unreality of its joyous calm, for the rhythm seems to exclude it from the central language of *Idomeneo*. The final chorus, No. 18, is in $\frac{12}{8}$, a metre Mozart used very rarely. Since the bars at the opening are alternatively piano and forte, this metre is audible – it is not two conflated bars of $\frac{6}{8}$ – and it contributes towards the hectic nature of the music. Within this field of associations it is no surprise to find the idyll at the start of Act III including the first whole aria in triple time (No. 19), and part of a duet in $\frac{3}{8}$ (the latter is used once more, out of deference to Raaff, in the middle section of 'Torna la pace').[9]

Many noticeable recurrent features are neither frequent nor consistent enough to contribute to the interpretation of the opera as a whole; yet they too may add something to its unique flavour. One which seems more a question of 'tinta' – of a consistency of expressive gesture rather than a decodable sign – is motive D, defined (Ex. 1.4) as a fairly normal chromatic embellishment of a descending arpeggio. In No. 2 Idamante's mellifluous anguish emerges in this kind of shape over the extended cadence (bars 60, 63; it is smoothed out in the reprise). As orchestral tremolando, the figure accompanies the chorus 'Numi pietà'. It occurs in the bass of R.6 and, as a vivid image of despair, on strings in R. 7, both before and after the precipitate exit of Idomeneo (Ex. 9.5).[10] This motive is less conspicuous during the second act. A number of chromatic figures might be related to D, even, perhaps, the melodic curve of the second phrase of 'Se il padre perdei' (see Ex. 7. 1a), but this is a Mozartian fingerprint.[11]

There are obvious limits to what a composer can do to avoid such resemblances when fired to employ chromatic means for local expressiveness in a dramatic work. However, motive D is clearer in the third act (R. 20), and also influences the expressive closing stages of the quartet, in imitation between the violins (from bar 139). Its apotheosis, intriguingly enough, coincides with that of 'motive C' during No. 23 bars 83–4. Nevertheless, this is no 'leitmotif', nor are there cogent reasons for believing that Mozart's use of this figure was intentionally cross-referential, except within R. 7b.

The glissandi in motive A at the start of the overture can be detected in other passages whose expressive force results from notes almost too fast to be distinguished, but which have no apparent

Example 9.5

connection with the mood of the overture. Coupled with more complex harmony, these slides become agitated, part of the storm music, in the last bars of No. 4 and the chorus (Ex. 9. 6a). A diatonic context is restored in the march (No. 8, from bar 9). This figure is audibly related to the musical equivalent of gooseflesh in Idamante's response to his first rejection by Idomeneo (R. 7b, Ex. 9.6b). Similar forms appear near the end of the horrorstruck chorus No. 17 and in the recitative which precedes Elettra's final aria, just as she begins: 'Oh smania! Oh furie! Oh disperata Elettra!' (see Ex. 11.10). Yet this is certainly no 'storm motive'. With the realism which was the aim of much late 18th-century staging, Mozart would hardly have wasted effort on anything so tautological.

Perhaps the tendency – it is hardly more than that – towards dislocation of tonality or an expansion of the toleration of dissonance, emerges fleetingly but most memorably in a few passages of recitative where the instrumental commentary seems to take over the mind of a character and convey meanings beyond the halting ejaculations of the verbal text. Before Elettra's first aria, she is reduced to the vaguest exclamations ('O sdegno! O smanie! O duol!' (O despite, o desire, o sorrow)): the strings pile up a chromatically

Example 9.6

inflected fifth g-d beneath her top g″, then descend, over the same restricted interval, in chromatic harmony of shivering iridescence.[12] Another outstandingly expressive orchestral invention emerges in Arbace's scena 'Sventurata Sidon'. He looks to heaven and finds an illusory gleam of hope. The spiralling violins both seduce and, in a painful contrapuntal collision, pierce the vision; twice Mozart accents two clashing adjacent semitones (f♮, f♯, g).[13]

These daring passages involve no unequivocal motivic cross-reference, but in each, reinforced by the existence of the others, we sense the unique character of *Idomeneo*. They stand out in defiance of the decorous musical language of the time; each of them goes well beyond the normal *opera seria* composer's reaction to a situation demanding heightened expression. Even if they are related to characteristic 'topics' which were widely understood, they constitute the transformation of generalised references into highly original and acute new images. They are Mozart's equivalent to Berlioz's tomb scene (*Roméo et Juliette*), the 'bitonality' of Strauss's *Also sprach Zarathustra*, even Wagner's *Tristan* chord: rationalised by theory after the event, they must have shocked early audiences more concerned with entertainment than pity and terror, and they retain their fascination and power undimmed.

Key-schemes in *Idomeneo*

Helmut Federhofer distinguishes two possible approaches to large-scale tonal organisation in number operas such as *Idomeneo*: 'Does the choice of tonalities only follow a musical-architectonic principle, as in cyclic instrumental forms, or does it, also or exclusively, serve a dramatic purpose?'[1] This is not the place to question the assumption that the choice of tonalities in cyclic instrumental forms does, in fact, follow such a principle. This choice, however, is intrinsically less likely to signify in opera, where the time-span is greater, the number of keys used for self-contained musical sections is far wider, and where poetic, visual, and dramatic considerations will be uppermost in the spectators' minds, as they surely were in the authors'.

Nevertheless, *Idomeneo*, like other Mozart operas, has been analysed in terms of tonal schemes, approached from both points of view: the architectonic and the dramatic. In practice, the two are interlinked.[2] Large-scale tonal schemes depend on the keys of whole numbers. In performance these are only tenuously, if at all, related to each other, since they are generally separated by recitative (or, in operas like *Die Zauberflöte*, speech). A simple juxtaposition of related keys (as between Nos. 13 and 14, from G to C) appears semantically insignificant through its very ordinariness, as would related keys connected by short and simple recitatives. Where the recitative is longer and wider-ranging tonally (as is frequently the case in *Idomeneo*) the numbers are decisively separated, and apparently striking key-relations cannot be heard: hence in performance, key-relations between successive but separated numbers are hardly ever rhetorically effective. Really recognisable and striking juxtapositions of keys, as when the final chorus bursts joyously (or crudely) forth in D major following Idomeneo's abdication, are unusual, and the symphonic join of Nos. 4 and 5 – see chapter 11 – is in every way exceptional.

It is generally held to be an axiom that Mozart's later operas have a 'tonic' or principal key, although *Idomeneo* is unusual in that every act ends in the key of the overture, D major. Nevertheless, the key-structure of *Idomeneo* appears weaker overall than in the da Ponte comedies, precisely because of such devices as the final sequence of B♭ and D major which preclude a steady development towards the last tonal goal, and because none of the acts ends with a lengthy finale which itself is tonally closed.

Nevertheless, several critics have found expressive or structural significance in the tonalities of *Idomeneo*. Liebner asserts that every recurrence of D, major or minor, coincides with a significant turning-point in the action.[3] Undoubtedly, in *Idomeneo*, such D major pieces as 'Fuor del mar' and Idomeneo's recitative 'Eccoti in me, barbaro Nume! il reo' are turning-points, but others, such as the ballets at the ends of the first and final acts, are not: and several principal turning-points use other keys, such as Idomeneo's confession of the name of the victim (C and G minor), Idamante's entry for sacrifice (A♭), and the voice of the god (C minor). Heartz points to Idomeneo's moment of recognition in R. 7 ('Spietatissimi Dei!') and Idamante's triumph over the monster in Act III as dependent for their effect on the returns of D major. But the latter is a theatrical device (off-stage trumpets and drums) which, given that No. 26 is in F, could scarcely have used any other key; the alternative 'trumpet key', C, is too close to F to be as effective *at that moment*. There is little question of larger-scale structure here, or of the choice of D major contributing dramatic insight. In the recognition scene, D major is marked by the orchestral entry after simple recitative, and by a violin arpeggio resembling the bass arpeggios of the overture (bar 23: note also the D major outburst in the sacrifice scene, No. 27, bar 35, at 'Barbaro, iniquo fato!'). In these recitatives, however, D major is a chord rather than a tonality, so the significance of such cross-references is far from clear. It is not self-evident that the brief recurrence of a key, even with a modest resemblance to an earlier occurrence, explains anything (such as that Idomeneo has realised that the sacrificial victim is his son) which is not apparent from less esoteric factors, such as the words and gestures of the characters, or indeed prior knowledge (which Varesco and Mozart assumed) of how the scene must proceed.[4]

The only key besides D major for which comparable significance might be claimed is C minor (see also chapter 11, below). It is supported by motivic cross-reference between its appearances in Acts I and III, but it remains an open question whether these would not signify just as strongly if Elettra's third aria, like her first, had been in D minor. Although it would be unusual for a character to have two arias in the same key, this would have presented no tonal difficulty; indeed, Mozart's last version of Elettra's Act III recitative, designed for performance without the aria, ends in D minor, a choice designed, perhaps, to underline her isolation from what follows (Idomeneo's recitative in E♭) by means of a tonal *non-sequitur*.

Several critics have drawn attention to an interrupted progression of fifths in Act II, starting with 'Fuor del mar': No. 12 is in D, No. 13 in G, No. 14 in C, No. 16 in F, but No. 15 in E.[5] In itself, descending fifths are the most self-effacing (and relaxed) way of linking pieces, since the first key acts as dominant to the second (cf. also Nos. 24–5). The idea that this sequence is interrupted by the delusory calm of No. 15 ('Placido e il mar') is undeniably seductive. But the attempt to hear the fifths is frustrated, in every case except at the junction of Nos. 13 and 14, by foreground detail. The recitative provides smooth progressions between the remote keys of Nos. 14 and 15, and Nos. 15 and 16 (although a new scene begins at this point with the entry of Idomeneo and Idamante). And No. 16, as it happens, disguises its tonality, F, by opening on a chord of D minor. A dramatic, rather than purely tonal, reading would emphasise the connections between Nos. 13 and 15, numbers concerned with Elettra's short-lived happiness, and the lack of connections between Nos. 13 and 14 and Nos. 14 and 16, pairs of movements ostensibly related by dominant-tonic progressions. Dramatically, too, No. 12 ('Fuor del mar') is linked to No. 11 ('Se il padre perdei') through the motives of the preceding recitative, but there is no tonal relation (E♭ goes to D: see chapter 8, p. 113, above).

The choice of tonalities in *Idomeneo* cannot be shown to be consistent either as structure or as a symbolic system. The best case for the latter, apart from Elettra's relationship with C minor, is that Idamante repeatedly enters to a chord of B♭; the only exception is his last entry, robed for sacrifice. It is not easy to perceive a serious reason for this fact (see chapter 9, p. 120, above), and I know of no method of ensuring its audible recognition that can compare with the ability of a listener to notice melodic or harmonic motives. It is certainly intriguing that Idamante's last aria (No. 27a/27) is in the 'tonic', D major, and Idomeneo's is in B♭ (No. 30a/31); but the dramatic reversal of roles, obvious by other means, is what matters. The tonal reversal can be no more than an abstract symbol which the composer makes no effort to communicate (indeed, he was prepared to omit both these arias).

It is, in short, far more likely that Mozart chose the tonalities of the set pieces without an eye to overall unity; and there is no really sufficient basis for regarding the keys as possessing much expository or explanatory function. In choosing keys, vocal tessitura must have been a prime consideration; instrumentation another. Indeed, it is worth asking in what sense 'Fuor del mar' (No. 12) and 'No, la morte io non pavento' (No. 27a) are significantly in the same key. They are widely separated, and have different forms, tempi, themes, and instrumentation, which leaves little but the absolute pitch of the tonics to connect them. 'Fuor del mar' lacks only clarinets and the second pair of horns from the fullest instrumentation of the opera; it is isolated by this sonority from its surroundings, whereas 'No, la morte' blends with them, adding only oboes and horns, sparingly used, to the strings of the obbligato recitative. 'Fuor del mar' is in D for the same reason that the overture and ballets are; in this key, trumpets and drums could be used (the only other possibility in *Idomeneo* is C), and violins, because of the disposition of their open strings, sound correspondingly brilliant. The E major of 'Placido e il mar' returns for 'Zeffiretti lusinghieri', which also speaks of kindly breezes, but the choice is equally validated by sonority, notably the contributions of horns, clarinets, and strings, and by its suitability for this particular melodic substance within the vocal range comfortable for Dorothea Wendling.[6]

Motivic 'structure' and expression

What alternatives are there to the beguiling but (I believe) empty tonal structures discussed above? One might seek coherence in the use of motives, which are far easier to recognise after a lapse of time than keys. Motives are also problematic within a number opera, but the quest for meaning seems worth pursuing, and recurring motives in *Idomeneo* have been an object of critical exploration at least since Dent drew attention to motive C from the overture (see above, p. 119). A careful reading of the score reveals over thirty passages which can be referred to (though not identified with) this motive, although several quite lack the 'tragic import' recognised by Dent (it is difficult to discern, unless we assume an elaborate sense of irony, in the final ballet).[7] Allusions to motive C vary widely in their exactness and the extent to which it is reasonable to suppose that they can be perceived as allusions. The motive is initially characterised by a dotted rhythm, a sforzando, a rapid descent complementing the dotted value, and the repetition of the lowest note. Cairns, who does not claim that C is a leitmotif, derives from it part of the vocal line of 'Fuor del mar'.[8] Floros, consistent with his claim that C is a motive signifying 'Idamante' or 'sacrifice', concentrates on instrumental statements; but some have little more in common with the original than a descending pattern (although they do, of course, occur at suitable moments in the drama).[9] The wind figure in Ilia's aria in Act II (Ex. 7.1b) has also been associated with C, the rhythmic resemblance here overcoming the absence of the descending direction.

Many instances are more persuasive. In forms which can be readily identified, motive C appears twelve times in Ilia's first aria, after 'Un greco adorerò', accompanying 'D'ingrata al sangue mio' ('shall I love a Greek? Ungrateful to my birth'). The reference to Idamante is still more open in the duet No. 20a; motive C occurs only once, at 'Lo sposo mio sarai tu' ('You [Idamante] shall be my husband'). In No. 23 it occurs five times, as Idomeneo reveals the name of the victim (bars 78–84), and in No. 27 three times as Idamante expresses his willingness to be sacrificed (bars 19–24); and it is built into No. 30, in which Idomeneo hands over his kingdom to Idamante.

These instances rule out Dent's narrow association with the love of Ilia and Idamante, and make plausible Floros's (and Heartz's) identification with Idamante and by extension with the central dramatic motive, the sacrifice.[10] There are also clear references in Idamante's first aria (No. 2, bars 32 and 103) and in Idomeneo's (No. 6, bars 27 and 29), when he anticipates meeting the ghost of his future victim. Several instances, however, are less obviously audible or related to Idamante: they include remote allusions in Elettra's music, in the chorus which ends Act II ('Corriamo, fuggiamo'), and in the march and chorus which end Act I.[11]

Motive C is not the only motive which seems to acquire significance as the drama proceeds. The opening arpeggio of the overture (motive A) and the closing chromatic shape (essentially a descending arpeggio enriched with neighbour-notes) have been traced in the opera. The arpeggio is a natural musical response to ideas of authority and majesty, and recurs most evidently at the start of the High Priest's scene, No. 23. It would be going too far to assimilate every ascending arpeggio, even with some rhythmic similarity, to the same idea (see, for instance, Idamante's first aria at bar 73); such things have an immediate gestural significance which renders cross-reference a minor consideration.[12] The chromatic shape in Idamante's recitative after the recognition is certainly remarkable in expression; it is less certain what benefit accrues from identifying it with the closing shape of the overture (Ex. 1.4, motive D). However, such things contribute to the general unity of expressive means, the 'colorito', of *Idomeneo*.

A complex of ideas related to Ilia perhaps refers to her crucial role in the dénouement. It arises in the new motive of the last bars of the overture (Ex. 1.4, motive E). A similar double neighbour-note figure above the mediant is the central melodic motive of perhaps the strangest bars in the entire opera, near the opening of No. 23; here two bars in A♭ intervene after a majestic opening in C major, with no connection other than silence. The continuation is equally foreign, instrumentally and thematically if not tonally. Such disjunction in all musical dimensions demands explanation; and it may perhaps lie in the motivic complex, which is also represented in the final bars of Act II, which parallel the end of the overture and recur at the same pitch as the first motivic gesture of Act III, the main theme of Ilia's aria, No. 19. It may also be associated with Ilia's aria in Act II (see Ex. 7.1), Arbace's monologue (R. 22b), and, after the enigmatic reference in No. 23, with the sacrifice scene (No. 27).

I hazard that this network of motives, which extends somewhat further than this, may be connected with the ultimate point of the drama, the reconciliation of the temporal and divine orders through the completion, or remission, of the sacrifice.[13] It is surely true, as Liebner observes, that 'Neither earlier nor later in Mozart's dramatic works do we come across such a thorough application of this technique [of recurring musical thoughts]'.[14] It is also true that the technique is not that of leitmotif proper, for the motives when first heard cannot be construed. In Wagner, significant motives stand out from the musical texture at their first appearances even if their precise connotation ('sword', 'Siegfried', and so on) is only revealed later. Mozart originally slipped motive C in as a counterpoint to a

Example 10.1

No. 23 Largo

No. 19 Grazioso

R. 22 Adagio

No. 27 Largo

chromatic surge (Ex. 1.1b) which he hardly uses again; only in the transition and coda of the overture does it play a major role, and it is Ilia's first aria which makes it extraneous to the overture and stimulates the search for further occurrences. Those in Act III justify one's feeling that it is important, but it is the accumulation of associations rather than any translatable significance for any one occurrence, which conveys meaning beyond, or beneath, the words.

Similarly, the 'reconciliation' complex begins as a simple cadence; when, however, after linking Acts II and III it forms the opening of No. 19, it too begins to accumulate significance. In the end it is associated with Ilia as the redeeming figure whose selfless love brings about reconciliation of father and son, king and god. This is certainly a heavy weight for conventional material to bear, when it is never quite the principal idea of a major musical section (whereas motive C certainly is the principal idea in a number of passages). Yet the eloquence of this material is undeniable.

When building an opera, Mozart studied plot, text, and per-formers, and bore in mind elements which we cannot recover: the stage design, acting style, the reaction of the performers (and of patrons, like Karl Theodor and Joseph II) to the new music. He appears to have 'fixed' set numbers and then connected them by recitatives, the tonality of the set numbers having been chosen for vocal, instrumental, and rhetorical effectiveness rather than structure.

The breakdown of any semblance of tonal order in Act III (not that Acts I and II possess much more than a semblance) argues neither haste nor a failure of aesthetic vision; nor is it the inevitable result of the violent reversals of the plot. It may, however, be a symbol of these reversals.

Cumulation, continuity, and contrast, expressed by a strong degree of foreground coherence, are principles at work in most operas, including the earliest. Mozart uses every audible means available – among which tonal structures are hardly to be included – to realise a dramatic goal in which music plays the major articulative role. I do not dispute Craig Ayrey's suggestion (chapter 11, p. 142, below) that tonal relationships add to understanding; nothing in such a complex masterpiece is to be rejected as irrelevant without careful evaluation. These comments on tonality and motives are not meant negatively, they are only intended to continue their evaluation, begun by others. Mozart's own recorded thoughts about both *Idomeneo* and *Die Entführung* concern structure only in so far as they refer to longueurs and matters of proportion, the latter, of course, a vital part of the analytical and aesthetic evaluation of any opera. But whether or not Mozart deliberately provided tonal and motivic clues to his intentions, we should chiefly assess the results, and any other part of his operas, in the light of what he surely considered very closely, their dramatic significance.

II Elettra's first aria and the storm scene

CRAIG AYREY

The most remarkable feature of Elettra's first aria ('Tutte nel cor vi sento', Act I, Scene 6, No. 4), much commented on by Mozart scholars, is the modulation to C minor in bar 77. This key, decidedly remote from the tonic D minor, appears at the beginning of the reprise of this binary sonata form (without a development section) at the point where the return to the tonic is expected. Indeed, Mozart heightens this sense of expectation by approaching C minor from the relative major, F, but interrupts a conventional progression to the dominant A major (and thence to D) by introducing a diminished seventh chord with fermata in bar 76. This chord is harmonically ambiguous: it may resolve either to C minor as in the score, or with the A♭ notated enharmonically as the augmented sixth G♯, to an A major chord, the dominant of D. Ex. 11.1 shows the two interpretations of the chord and their resolutions.

Example 11.1

bars 76–7

The aural ambiguity of the chord lies in the fact that it can be understood only retrospectively, in this case when we hear C minor in the following bar. Mozart exploits this property in the recitatives of *Idomeneo*, where the volatile emotions of the characters are most often presented (see chapter 9, p. 120, above). But the chord has a special expressive power and meaning in arias or ensembles in which there is normally greater unity of expression and idea. (Significantly, the diminished seventh plays a crucial role in delineating the characters' fluctuating and diverse emotions in the quartet,

137

No. 21.) According to its context, then, the diminished seventh is 'marked for consciousness': together with its resolution to C minor, it presents a problem of structural ambivalence and discontinuity on various levels within Elettra's first aria that can be explained only in terms of character and dramatic purpose.

The diminished seventh chord has a formal function generated by Mozart's deployment of the two four-line stanzas of the text (see below) within the binary sonata structure.

Tutte nel cor vi sento,	In my heart I feel you all,
furie del crudo averno,	Furies of bitter Hades,
lunge a sì gran tormento	far from such fierce torment
amor, mercè, pietà.	are love, mercy, or pity.
Chi mi rubò quel core,	Let her who stole that heart,
quel che ha tradito il mio,	which has betrayed mine,
provin' dal mio furore	feel my fury
vendetta e crudeltà.	and cruel revenge.

Both stanzas are sung in the exposition, the first set as the first theme in the tonic, the second in the relative major with a new chromatic melodic figure (bar 40) related to an earlier motive (bar 31) setting lines three and four of the first stanza (see Ex. 11.2).

Example 11.2

The presentation of all the textural and melodic material in the exposition achieves the concentration of expression appropriate to Elettra's highly charged emotion; maintaining this intensity obviates the need for a formal development. Yet, a renewal of expressive force in the reprise is required that a simple recapitulation cannot provide. Thus, the resolution of the diminished seventh chord on C minor has a strategic role in heightening the temperature of the return of Elettra's opening couplet by raising the expectation that the textual and thematic reprise is simultaneously the beginning of a tonal development. The technique here is similar to Haydn's 'false recapitulation' technique, except that in this case, the deception

turns out to be the thing itself. And the effect, of course, is quite
different from that in Haydn's sonata forms: in the aria, the dramatic effect of the reprise a tone lower than expected is of Elettra
containing her fury almost literally under her breath, after which
her anger escalates in the three arpeggiated ascents (not two as in
the exposition) leading to the tonic thirteen bars later (bar 90; see
Ex. 11.3). Harmonic ambiguity is therefore the agent of formal
ambiguity, and these structural features are the technical basis of
the power of Mozart's characterisation. Elettra's furious frustration
at the point of reprise is communicated by Mozart's carefully
placed aural correlative of this emotion, and in the larger context
of the opera this detail becomes a symptom of ambivalence and
fragmentation in Mozart's construction of her character.

Example 11.3

William Mann notes that the reprise 'apparently begins in the
wildly foreign key of C minor (relevant however to the next chorus)
which, having caused a shock, is quickly replaced by the home key
of D minor'.[1] Mann's parenthetical reference to the chorus, the
storm scene, is in fact the first clue to the larger dramatic purpose
of Mozart's tonal procedure in the aria, since apart from the
transition from aria to chorus (traversing the change of scene in
the libretto, without change of tempo), C minor is the most
obvious relation between the two numbers. The issue, though, is
the significance of these and other connections: the explanation
lies in Elettra's character as presented by Varesco and in Mozart's
interpretation of her function in the drama – that is, in her musico-
dramatic characterisation through large-scale tonal structure and
motivic relationships.

The 'drama' of Elettra

Elettra first appears in a short recitative (R. 4) beginning in C major in which she admonishes Idamante for freeing the Trojan prisoners: 'Prence, signor, tutta la Grecia oltraggi; tu proteggi il nemico' (Prince, my lord, you offend all Greece; you protect the enemy). This statement contains the seeds of the ambivalence of Elettra's character: it is here that what can be called the 'drama of Elettra' begins. Although we have been told in Ilia's opening recitative that Elettra is her rival in love for Idamante, Elettra challenges Idamante from the outset for both personal and political reasons. As she makes clear in her second recitative (Scene 6), she wishes to break the bond between Idamante and Ilia (whom she describes as a 'schiava Trojana', a Trojan slave) and to preserve the traditional antagonism between Greece and Troy. This dimension of her character shows her to be the representative of the old order and allied with Idomeneo, in so far as he puts political necessity (his survival as king) above personal considerations (Idamante's life). After the mistaken report of Idomeneo's death at sea, Elettra finds herself in a world in which the distinction between the personal and the political is blurred, and potentially erased by the bond of love.

Such a dilemma is conventional in *opera seria*, and in this respect Elettra is a stock character, presented by Mozart in a schematic way. She is given three arias. The first in D minor ('Tutte nel cor') and the last in C minor ('D'Oreste, d'Aiace') are rage arias, while the second ('Idol mio') is a simple statement of love for Idamante, in G major. This generic scheme, representing starkly the extremes of Elettra's character, has a dramatic purpose. While she does little to advance the plot, Elettra does embody the conflict of the personal and the political in its most elementary form. In contrast to Idomeneo's response to his similar dilemma, Elettra calls upon the guardians of conventional, political morality in the first of her two minor-key arias, and on the tormented heroes Orestes and Ajax in the second. But her anger is fuelled from a personal source, her love for Idamante, given full expression in the major-key aria. Since she lacks the emotional pliancy of Ilia and the humanity of Idamante, Elettra belongs to a different, harsher world of dichotomy and dilemma. Like Idomeneo, but more directly, she is associated with the mythological realm (palpable in the opera as the springboard of the plot), a connection revealed most clearly in the relation of her first aria to the storm scene. As the aria ends with Elettra's threat of vengeance upon Ilia for stealing Idamante's heart ('Chi mi rubò quel core, quel che ha tradito il mio'), the music moves without a break across the change of scene to the resurgence of the storm, a transition that cannot have a dramatic motivation in the plot. We have been informed earlier of the storm in which Idomeneo is thought drowned: indeed, it is this fact that occasions Elettra's outburst of fury in the aria. If we are to credit Varesco with any dramatic skill, then it must be concluded – as by Mozart – that the 'reprise' of the storm (but here portrayed in the music for the first time, No. 5) is a poetic device which functions as a physical representation of Elettra's personal feelings: the Furies of Hades are made real.² Considered as a symbolic manifestation of her threat of vengeance, the storm is the first demonstration in the opera of Elettra's access to the supramundane. This type of symbolism is both archaic and modern in the period: it is typical of both the *tragédie lyrique* (the source of the *Idomeneo* libretto) and of early Romantic literature, as the 'pathetic fallacy'.

The following recitative (Act I, Scene 8) restores order and calm: Idomeneo enters, declaring 'Eccoci salvi alfin', and the music moves from the turbulent C minor of the storm to E♭ major. Elettra returns to the prospect of revenge in the quartet with the words 'Quando vendetta avrò?' (bars 31–4), in a chromatic progression to the dominant; and after the four characters meditate on their various misfortunes ('Soffrir più non si può'), the drama moves towards the realisation of Idomeneo's vow to Neptune to sacrifice Idamante for his own life. Elettra's third, exit aria follows Idamante's reprieve by the Oracle. Here, having been thwarted by the gods, she threatens suicide: 'Squarciatemi il core, ceraste, serpenti, o un ferro il dolore in me finerà' (Tear out my heart, vipers, serpents, or a sword shall end my pain). She then leaves the stage to Idomeneo who announces in E♭ major: 'Popoli. A voi . . . Pace v'annunzio' (see chapter 12, below).

These three sections define the stages of the drama of Elettra, each involving a threat of violence, first to Ilia, then in the quartet requesting vengeance from heaven, and finally towards herself in suicide. But each threat has a similar context, emphasised by Mozart's key scheme. Except in the quartet, where the context is chromatic, Elettra's threats of violence always occur in C minor, followed by the symbolic intervention of the supernatural in the first two (the storm scene, and Idamante's slaying of the monster); and according to the peripeteia of classical tragedy, her exit aria is preceded by the Oracle (No. 28).[3] Thus Elettra's reversal of fortune is represented also by a reversal of the order of events. Each of the C minor sections is followed by a restoration of order in E♭ major with the appearance of Idomeneo. The tonal contexts of the three sections are shown in Table 11.1.

This scheme defines the extremes of Elettra's character: her address to Idamante and her love aria are both in major and are related as tonic (C) and dominant (G). The predominant aspect of her personality is defined by the minor key numbers (including the storm scene), between which the second aria in G major acts as a dominant major interlude. However, the scheme is not closed or self-contained as a large-scale tonal progression. Instead, its thrust is the descent harmonically from major to minor, and tonally from D major to C minor, as a symbol of Elettra's descent to the depths, to Hades, the world to which she most naturally belongs. Such a reading of large-scale symbolic tonal relations raises difficult interpretative issues. Clearly, the tonic-dominant relation of C major/minor and G major cannot be perceived in performance, and is in any case disturbed by the intervention of the D minor of Elettra's first aria: the most immediately expressive features are the contrasts of major and minor, tempo and instrumentation (the G major aria uses strings alone). In fact, the apparently factitious nature of the key relations presented in Table 11.1 represents the type of structural analysis recently challenged by James Webster, as the 'myth of musical unity' in Mozart.[4] But Webster and like-minded critics (who begin at the latest with Tovey) ignore the fact that, once stated, such analysis can modify the nature of our understanding of a work (and even our perception of it in performance).

That this understanding is informed by an interpretation of structural relations (an interpretation that, by definition, can be only one of many) does not invalidate, necessarily, the 'myth' the interpretation promotes. In this particular example, the large-scale tonal structure, based in the C/G polarity, is pertinent precisely because of the elements for which it cannot account – the 'restoration' to E♭ major, and the D minor aria. The key of the latter reveals the febrile nature of Elettra's rage simply by its tenuous position within the tonal framework. While the C minor reprise disrupts tonal structure within the aria, the disruption of the larger tonal scheme by the tonic key of the aria itself can be interpreted as a symbol of Elettra's potentially disruptive role in the plot, and her negative intentions (vengeance and cruelty) in a moral climate in which love

Table 11.1

Act/scene	I/1	I/6	I/7	I/8	II/4	III/3	III/7			III/scena ultima
Number	R. 4a 'Prence, signor'	No. 4 'Tutte nel cor'	No. 5 'Pietà'	Recit. 'Eccoci'	No. 13 'Idol mio'	No. 21 'Andrò, ramingo e solo'	Recit. 27 'Sire'	No. 28 (recit)	No. 29a 'D'Oreste, d'Aiace'	No. 30 'Popoli', '...'
Character	Elettra	Elettra	Chorus	Idomeneo	Elettra	Quartet	Arbace	La voce	Elettra	Idomeneo
Key	C minor (→F major)	D minor	C minor →	Eb major	G major	Eb major	D major (→Eb major)	C minor	C minor → Eb major	Eb major
Section	1				2		3			

and fidelity are the supreme virtues. Similarly, the 'resolutions' to Eb major, representing the restoration of order, contextualise the key of C minor associated with the forces beyond the control of the mortal characters. (C minor is the key of the Oracle, too.) Although there is no need to suggest that Mozart refers to a fixed system of key symbolism, as in the baroque 'doctrine of affections' (*Affektenlehre*), the correlation of key (or chord) and dramatic idea is striking in Elettra's personal 'drama'; whether all aspects of the tonal scheme are intentionally symbolic or are the products of small-scale dramatic effects is immaterial once the larger connections have been made. They may not be Mozart's intentional connections, but the proposition of such a large-scale structure is one way of demonstrating the expressive intensity of what is contained within it, an intensity that threatens to break the bounds of conventional formal and tonal structures.

Structural coherence in the first aria and chorus

The competing demands of emotive force and structural closure are most evident in Elettra's first scena. The aria begins on the dominant (prepared by the recitative) and lacks an introductory ritornello so that Elettra's first vocal entry coincides with the establishment of the tonic, D minor. This itself is a dramatic device: Elettra constantly appears *in medias res* in an explosion of emotion, as if her feelings can no longer be contained. (Her third aria in C minor begins similarly, but on the subdominant, F minor.) And the 'open' beginning is balanced by the end of the aria which modulates quickly from the D minor tonic of Elettra's final statement to the C minor of the storm, escalating her emotion into a physical cataclysm. The introduction to the aria (see Ex. 11.4) contains all the essential features of Elettra's musical characterisation: in particular, these eighteen bars present the chromatic procedures that take on expressive significance in Elettra's declamation.

The diminished seventh appears first in bars 5–6 and again in bars 11–12. Significantly, it is the same chord (untransposed) that effects the modulation to C minor (Ex. 11.1b). The context of the chord is important, too: the aria opens with a dominant pedal over which a chromatic harmonic progression begins with the arpeggiation of the tonic triad (bars 1–4), prolonging a larger line in the top voice, descending from A to D (beamed in Ex. 11.4). The role of the diminished seventh is extended in the progression

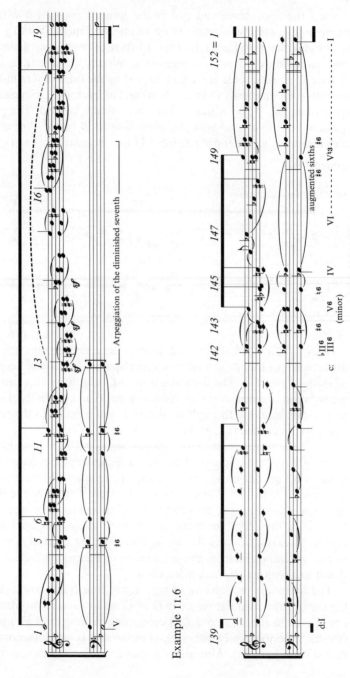

Example 11.4

Example 11.6

toward the first secure cadence in the tonic (bars 13–19) with a rising arpeggiation characterised by an implied $\frac{3}{4}$ metre (bars 13–16: see upward stems in Ex. 11.4). This structure of descending diatonic, and ascending chromatic, arpeggios is mirrored in Elettra's first statement, a rising tonic arpeggio followed by the original diminished seventh (this time with D in the bass) and a descending diminished triad (here C♯, E, G) within a dominant-seventh context. The progression ends in bar 30 with the resolution to D minor closing an ascending line in the top voice from D to F (beamed in Ex. 11.5).

Example 11.5

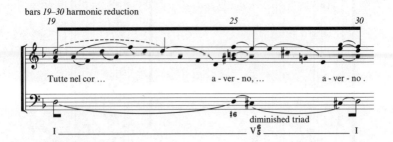

bars *19–30* harmonic reduction

These plunging descents and ascents both convey the general disturbance in Elettra's mind and are a specific large-scale motive of Hades ('averno'). The diminished seventh is now given a precise connotation: it occurs on the word 'averno' (bar 25, see Ex. 11.5), retains this meaning throughout the aria, and extends to the transition to the chorus (Ex. 11.6).

While the progression (bars 139–51) begins with the descents in thirds of bars 13–15, it now elaborates a descending chromatic turn in the top line, not an ascent as in the introduction. Furthermore, the passage ends with a chromatic descent from G to C in the flute and oboe (bars 149–52), simultaneously with a chromatic ascent in the strings, thus combining the two motivic ideas associated with Hades. Mozart introduces the storm, then, with the musical symbols of Hades, and emphasises the connection of Elettra's private emotional hell with its 'real' manifestation.

The harmonic progression in bars 142–9 is also important. It is the crux of the modulation from D to C, and contains two diminished sevenths (bars 143 and 145) connecting the chords of E♭ major (the flat supertonic in D, bar 142), G minor and F minor (becoming A♭ major in bar 147). Although the diminished-seventh sonority is

Example 11.7

retained, the function of these chords is modulatory rather than motivic: the sudden appearance of E♭ has dramatic import here because it is the final, summary example of a chromatic process begun in the vocal line in bar 31, the new musical idea setting the third line of Elettra's first stanza, 'lunge a sì gran tormento . . .' (Ex. 11.7a). There is a clear relation to the text here: 'lunge' (far) is represented by the E♭ major triad, distantly related to the tonic D. What appears as a chromatic inflection in the voice (E♭, D, C♯) therefore acquires a symbolic function through the transformation it effects in the harmonic structure.

Mozart extends this significance in the following bars, where the progression is repeated, then prolonged, at the words 'amor, mercè, pietà' (Ex. 11.7b; cf. Ex. 11.2). This passage is the first instance of melodic chromaticism in the aria and is the source of the chromatic turn in the top line of bars 140–1, a link that confirms the summarising function of the transition to the storm scene. Example 11.7b ends on the dominant (bar 37) from which a modulation begins, via an oblique harmonic progression, to the C major chord on which Elettra's second stanza begins (bar 40). The progression ascends chromatically in the melodic line, introducing an augmented sixth chord in bar 39, which in this context can be interpreted as a transformation of the diminished seventh (the D natural is lowered to D♭, Ex. 11.8c).

However, this chord has been prepared by the E♭ major chord (Ex. 11.7a, bars 31 and 33), which with the addition of the C♯ is an elaborate version of the augmented sixth; this type of chord also plays a crucial harmonic role in the transition to the chorus, bars 148 and 150, where it frames the dominant of C minor (Ex. 11.6, bar 149). The cadence in C minor, the key that establishes tonal and dramatic descent, is thus contextualised by the chords symbolic of Elettra's distress, completing a substructure in which the diatonicism of all the main formal sections of the aria – the orchestral introduction, the exposition of Elettra's first stanza, the beginning of the reprise, and the transition to the chorus – is encompassed by the two chromatic chord types. While it intensifies the sense of resolution, this substructure destabilises the tonality of the aria since both the diminished seventh and the augmented sixth are tonally ambiguous and have accrued dramatic significance. Harmonic and tonal resolution are construed as a tenuous stability to which Elettra clings as a psychological anchor: dramatic meaning and characterisation are therefore presented symbolically as tonal and harmonic ambiguity. A further dimension of this harmonic substructure is its relation to tonal structure. Except when the diminished seventh or augmented sixth is played over a dominant pedal, the bass of the progression descends a tone or a semitone (for example D♭ to C, bars 39–40), thus expressing in the small scale the large-scale descent from the D of the aria to the C minor of the chorus and – within the aria – the tonal context of the C minor reprise.

Elettra's second stanza ('Chi mi rubò quel core') begins with a rising version of the chromatic motive of the preceding bars, with the D♭ (bar 41 and later) producing another diminished seventh over a C pedal as Elettra considers Idamante's betrayal of her love. This is a further extension of the significance of the chord, established in bars 44–5 with the arpeggiation in the voice from b' to a♭". Subsequently, the A♭ itself is invested with dramatic meaning when it recurs on the word 'crudeltà' (bar 53). As the flattened third of F major, the A♭ acts as a large-scale chromatic inflection of the major triad, adding a further dimension to the topos of descent that grounds Mozart's presentation of the motives of pitilessness, vengeance, and cruelty.

The syncopated descents of the introduction (bars 13–15) reappear here in the orchestra (bars 48–52), creating a motivic link between the ideas informing the first stanza – torment and Hades ('tormento' and 'averno', connected by the half rhyme in the Italian) – and the informing ideas of the second stanza. Mozart picks up the poetic significance of Varesco's rhyme scheme here. The three crucial emotions ('pietà, 'vendetta', and 'crudeltà) are the only words in the text ending with '–a'. 'Pietà' and 'crudeltà' are most closely associated in this respect: they end each stanza and are the only *verso tronco* rhymes, but they are, of course, opposed as the poles of Elettra's character.⁵ (These distinctions are fused in the chorus where the multiple repetitions of 'Pietà' become a plea, almost a demand, for deliverance.) In the exposition, however, Mozart shifts the emphasis to 'vendetta' in response to the location of the word as an internal *verso piano* rhyme in the last line of the text, a duplication introduced by Varesco to emphasise the cumulative effect of negative emotions. In the reprise, though, chromaticism is transferred to the end of the line, to 'crudeltà' (bars 112–14 and 127–34), signalling a shift from intention (vengeance) to action (cruelty) as an aspect of Elettra's increasing resolve. In the exposition this chromatic process begins obliquely in bars 40–50, during the course of the progression from C to F (the relative major of D). Since C functions as the dominant of F, Elettra again begins a new phrase of expression in the middle of a harmonic structure, reflecting the similar procedures at the beginning of the exposition, and especially in the reprise, where C major functions tonally in a progression to the tonic D ($\flat$VII–V6–I) achieved in bar 90.

Example 11.8

Bar:	*1 19*		*40*	*48*		*76*	*77*		*90*	
1. Tonal structure D:	I			III			($\flat$VII)	V⁶	I	
	1st theme			2nd theme			1st theme			2nd theme
2. Formal structure	**EXPOSITION**						**REPRISE**			

Two tonal structures are therefore at work in the aria: the first, a conventional tonal structure outlining a large-scale cadential progression, the second a 'counterstructure' based in the lack of correspondence between formal-thematic structure and the primary tonal structure (see Ex. 11.8).⁶ Although this duality is exploited in Mozart's instrumental music (and extensively in Beethoven's), its disruption of normative tonal relations in the aria is not simply an example of a characteristic classical structural device. By locating the expression of Elettra's conflicting emotions in keys distant from D minor (C major, as the dominant of F, in the exposition; C minor in the reprise), Mozart establishes the subtonic as a counterpole to the tonic which dramatises the psychological contradictions of character. The full extent of this dramatic manipulation of tonality is confirmed later: the aria's counterstructure is a smaller-scale expression of the tonal scheme defining the 'drama of Elettra' (as shown in Table 11.1), which turns on the dramatic functions of C major and C minor.

A different type of complexity is present in the storm scene: texture and motivic correspondence are the loci of dramatic symbolism, while the tonal structure remains securely diatonic beneath the chromatic surface, avoiding the structurally disruptive tonal features of the aria. The textural and motivic complexity – produced by the *coro lontano* and *coro vicino*, the swirling arpeggios and forceful scales of the orchestra, and the intensity of expression inherent in the chromatic melodic movement and suspensions (e.g. bars 33–6) – is controlled by the concentrated tonal span uniting a correspondingly tight formal structure. The chorus is a binary form, but the second section (from bar 27) begins in the tonic, reproducing the harmonic progressions of the first section almost without modification. This is not unusual, and in this respect it represents the structural convention flouted so dramatically in the binary sonata structure of the aria.[7] But since the storm scene lacks a definite second thematic area, present in the aria, there is no internal symbolism of key or tonality. This, in fact, is unnecessary. Because the storm is effectively portrayed by texture and motive as the emanation of Elettra's fury, the scene performs an illustrative dramatic function that does not require the more complex procedures of the aria. The constraints of genre here are nevertheless turned to advantage in the contrast, for dramatic effect, of the chorus's structural unity with the discontinuous aspects of Elettra's aria.

However, if the tonal structure of the chorus is unremarkable, the thematic structure is distinctive. The second section opens with a new motive at the words 'In braccio a cruda morte' (Ex. 11.9a), so that the repetitive binary structure is disguised and intensified by the introduction of new, imitative, and sequential material which contrasts with the antiphonal homophony (overlaid with chromatic scales in the orchestra) of the first section, and gives the movement renewed impetus.

Example 11.9

This new theme has the same basic shape as the opening motive of
Elettra's exit aria (Ex. 11.9b), a connection that gives the chorus
both a retrospective and anticipatory function in the opera. While
losing the descending thirds on the first beat of the bar that relate
Elettra's first and last arias (compare Ex. 11.9b and c), the chorus
is retrospective motivically in retaining the triadic material of
Elettra's first phrase in 'Tutte nel cor' (Ex. 11.9c) but transformed
by shape and key. The connection with her aria in Act III is
therefore much stronger and is confirmed by the almost identical
orchestral motives in the introduction to the aria (bars 1–4) and
in bars 27–32 of the chorus where it occurs together with the 'In
braccio' motive (Ex. 11.10). Motivically *and* tonally, then, Elettra's
third aria functions as the conclusion of a long-range musico-
dramatic structure.

    Such a web of interrelationships confirms the large dimensions
of Mozart's characterisation of Elettra. She is portrayed not only
in the arias but, crucially, is revealed as a character of great power
whose ambitions are thwarted by the very supramundane forces
she calls to her aid. While she is able to call forth the physical
cataclysm of the storm, she is nevertheless powerless against love,
the specifically and uniquely human force in the opera. This
conflict can only be fully developed in a structure of symphonic
proportions, with all the tonal, formal, and thematic complexity
that this entails. Elettra's scena is the first example in *Idomeneo* of
Mozart's move toward structural continuity, transcending the

Example 11.10

Aria: D'Oreste, d'Aiace

Chorus No. 5

constraints of *opera seria* while using them to dramatic effect. If Elettra is a typical *seria* character, and as such conforms to the conventions of the genre, this conformity contains, but does not restrain, the expression of her complex psychology. Conflict within Elettra's character, rather than among her relations with others, is the primary source of dramatic conflict, explored and controlled by the manipulation of formal and tonal conventions. The dramatic potential of these techniques is fully realised in Mozart's later operas, most notably in the character of Donna Elvira in *Don Giovanni* in whom the conflict of love and duty is developed to expand a conventional *seria* role into a more flexible 'mezzo carattere'.[8] In *Idomeneo*, though, Mozart's treatment of Elettra forms a psychological and ideological sub-plot in which *opera seria* is nascent music drama.

12 *Conclusions*

Having considered *Idomeneo* historically and in terms of genre, and then of its standing throughout its two centuries of existence, and having tapped some of its potential for deep critical analysis, we are still a long way from exhausting what this opera has to offer. I shall conclude by attempting to tie up a few musical, dramatic, and generic loose ends, and making a few suggestions for an interpretation, which are not intended to be prescriptive (either for critical response or for staging), but which attempt to reconcile a contemporary and a modern view.

Modern interpretations of Mozart's first operatic masterpiece take their lead from Dent, whose general view was that its elevated tone restores to the theatre something essential to its spirit that modern drama – including Shakespeare and most opera – tends to evade. This is to restore to *Idomeneo*, in a positive light, the association with neo-classical drama which Hanslick used, mildly, to denigrate it (see p. 87, above). *Idomeneo* concerns the relationship between human and divine government, and a willingness to suspend disbelief in the ancient gods is essential. What, in the eighteenth or twentieth centuries of the Christian era, those old gods might signify, is a larger question, but nearly every human society has been based on a system of relationship between a perceived superhuman order and the ordering of human life itself: the theme is universal.

Hocquard has argued that Mozart 'recovers the dramaturgy of the Greek tragedians'.[1] Don Neville (chapter 5) argues that the divine background to the drama is less apparent in the Mozart opera than in its French source; but this objection applies only to the librettos. The potency of Neptune, within *Idomeneo*, lies in manifestations – tempest, ravening monster, oracle – both natural and supernatural, rather than through an anthropomorphic apparition on the model of a *deus ex machina*. *Tragédie lyrique* is too often inhabited by gods whose feelings are no different from those of the human characters: this rather frivolous dramatic pattern, by no means excluded from *Idomenée*, Varesco and Mozart managed to break.

Against this supernatural background, critics have found the characters bland – with the exception of the one least essential to the action, Elettra. Joseph Kerman, indeed, suggests that 'youth prevails by passivity'.[2] This, however, is hardly fair to Idamante, who slays the monster, or Ilia who intervenes at the crisis. As for Idomeneo, his actions are doomed to futility, but his music (especially 'Fuor del mar') does not make a passive impression. It may well be, as Kerman observes, that 'nothing becomes Idomeneo more than his abdication . . . although "Torna la pace" is certainly a very long aria and old-fashioned in cast, it is the most heartfelt of the three he sings'. Nevertheless, every action these characters take is under the shadow of an authority higher than that of Cretan society.

It follows that the common suggestion that *Idomeneo* is mainly concerned with the relationship of the father and son, interpreted in a post-Freudian way as a concern with infanticidal cannibalism, must be treated with scepticism.[3] As Hocquard observes, interpretation in terms of Mozart's biography 'illuminates nothing and only complicates the issues, for nothing in the reactions of Idamante towards his father displays anything other than unwavering affection'.[4] Interpretation in terms of father–son tension belittles the drama, in which the difficulties of this particular relationship (the two have not met for ten years) are not inherently psychological, but are a tragic misfortune resulting from an arrogant vow.

The story of Idomeneus is, of course, as much a sacrifice story as the Agamemnon (Iphigenia) and Jephtha stories; the earliest sources all, indeed, assume the consummation of the sacrifice. But a happy ending for *Idomeneo*, although only invented for this opera, is less artificial than when applied to its likely models. In the making of a drama, the violent accident of Fénelon's ending, essentially followed by Danchet, is hardly preferable to the unlikely suicide of an improbably over-noble Idamante favoured by Crébillon and Lemierre, modelled though it surely was on the submissiveness of the heroine in Racine's popular weepie, which became the source of Gluck's first French opera, *Iphigénie*. In ending by abdication and the reversal of roles between father and son, Varesco (or Seeau, or Mozart) found a way out of a dramatic impasse which leaves us, not harrowed by pity and terror, but relieved to find divine justice tempered by mercy.[5]

The main drawback of critical concentration on the father–son relationship is that it underrates the significance of Ilia. Mozart developed her role by three consistently masterly arias, none of which was cut (so far as is known) in any of his performances. In Danchet Ilione shows heroic stature at the end, but the Varesco–Mozart Ilia, freed of sexual pressure from the king, initiates the process of reconciliation (in 'Se il padre perdei'). At the crisis she voluntarily assumes the role of sacrifice from love of Idamante, and of all things connected with him; which by now include Idomeneo, Crete, and indeed 'Grecia', her father's enemy. This is encapsulated in the complex of 'reconciliation' motives (see chapter 10, p. 134, above) and in some recitative which, amazingly, shows that Mozart still had much in reserve (see chapter 9, p. 123, above). Hermann Abert wisely spoke of the '"äusseren" und "inneren" Handlung' – the outer and inner action – of *Idomeneo*.[6] The outer action is the visible operation of the plot, in which Idomeneo is the protagonist; the inner action is the development of character which leads to action, and Ilia is the protagonist. Idamante, of course, is the link between the two. Curiously, however, this scheme makes no mention of Elettra, whose role is fully equal to the others.

The libretto of *Idomeneo* may be overlong and pompous in language and versification; but it is impressive as a structure (see chapter 7, above). Precisely what responsibility Mozart had for this we cannot be sure, but there seems no reason to deprive Varesco, Seeau, and possibly Leopold Mozart, of some of the credit. Structure is not mere architecture, but a contribution to dramatic meaning: the larger political and religious dimension of the action is a vital part of it. If the gods were not real, there would be no point in the sacrifice: Idomeneo's rescue would have been merely lucky, and there would have been no obstacle to Idamante's escape at the end of Act II. One of Mozart's most readily recognised achievements in *Idomeneo* lies in making human feelings important within a divine framework, greatly assisted by its clear structure. His model, or Varesco's, was surely Gluck for whom divine interventions are arranged symmetrically: the two interventions of Amor in *Orfeo*, the oracle and intervention of Apollo in the 1767 *Alceste*, the two appearances of Kalchas in *Iphigénie en Aulide*, the divinely ordered storm and *dea ex machina* in *Iphigénie en Tauride*, which all correspond to the *pantomima* and Oracle in *Idomeneo*.[7]

Varesco's version brought one apparent obscurity, the role of Elettra, who for Kerman is 'as remote from the opera's true centre as Arbace'. The Elettra problem is not confined to the fact of her presence on the island, inexplicable as this is in terms of all the other tales of Agamemnon's unfortunate family. It is rather that she, finally, does nothing; even less than in Danchet (see chapter 5, p. 73, above). She is sometimes justified as a foil to Ilia: both princesses have lost their fathers, Ilia by the misfortunes of war, Elettra, equally deserving our sympathy, from a family murder. But we hear little of this; it hardly affects her thinking at all. Instead she is obsessed both with Idamante and her own dignity, thus setting in relief the selflessness and essential goodness of Ilia. Elettra herself, when her rival intervenes between their loved one and the sacrificial sword, mutters: 'O qual contrasto!' We can have only limited sympathy for Elettra.

Yet to act as a foil is hardly sufficient cause for her musical and dramatic weight; and nor is Hocquard's conception of her, as a kind of Greek chorus.[8] Our modern sense of the grandeur of this conception, the subject of chapter 11, owes something to extraneous knowledge; we know Elettra as the daughter of Klytemnestra, whether the Clytemnestre of Gluck's *Iphigénie en Aulide*, which Mozart probably knew, or Strauss's *Elektra* which we know today. Elettra is that Elektra: the Elektra of Sophocles, so wronged that she can contemplate with lust the killing of her own mother. It is not really possible to suppress this knowledge when watching *Idomeneo*. And why, indeed, should we? For this knowledge assists in understanding her function within Mozart's opera.

Elettra's brooding revives the drama at a moment in Act I when it has veered perilously close to blandness: the entrance of Arbace and the reactions of Idamante and Ilia to his report of Idomeneo's death are expressed with dignity, but strike few sparks. Elettra's interpretation of the news, coming upon her discovery of the freeing of the Trojans, makes her the human equivalent of the storm which is battering the coast of Crete; hence Mozart's inspiration of running her first aria into the chorus of drowning sailors, a conception for which there is no reason to credit the librettist. In the light of Act I, Elettra's 'Idol mio' has a sinister calm as if at the heart of the storm; and her repressed fury in the Quartet, where her desire for vengeance is controlled by social decorum, makes inevitable her explosion of rage after the god has granted Idamante to Ilia.

While Ilia is formed before our eyes and ears into a heroine of human determination and noble self-effacement, Elettra retains the stature of a mythological creature. Her final recitative and aria, in their original form, are remarkable even by the standards of *Idomeneo*. She intrudes after the radiant wind chord haloes the reactions of the other characters, and the orchestra is obsessed with the 'slide' motive reminiscent of the passage in which her first aria merged into the storm (see Exx. 9.6a and 11.10). Mozart deploys contrasts of tempo, abrupt harmonic shifts, and an exceptionally full instrumentation for this recitative; in the shorter recitative which he probably used in his performances (*MW*, 359; *NMA*, 474), trumpets and drums burst in, overturning the ascending D major arpeggio of the overture.

In the original and longer version (*MW*, 355; *NMA*, 569) her cries of 'misera' are accompanied by a new violin figure suggestive of the punishments inflicted by the Eumenides, while the voice is echoed in several layers by the woodwind: the subsequent triplet figure (bar 19) directly recalls the scene in Gluck's *Iphigénie en Aulide* where her father Agamemnon also faces the wrath of the Eumenides. Later a solemn Andante (bar 44) conjures up the tormented shade of Orestes, and a melting conclusion blends into the aria itself. This is one of the most magnificent of Mozart's recitatives, and the aria 'D'Oreste, d'Aiace' is its worthy sequel. The Eumenides are in the foreground now, their angry hissing represented by the violins in octaves, while the divided violas fill out the texture with another motive; all this provides a seething backcloth for the voice's sweeping melodic paragraphs. Woodwind again echo the voice, but inexactly, to greater expressive effect, in the setting of the second quatrain (Ex. 12.1).[9] The aria ends with challenging syncopations rising to c^3 and a hysterically cackling descent; the coda returns to the hissing motive in a tutti which breathes aggression, before ending with a sigh of the 'Idamante' motive. This harsh C minor is supported by full orchestration, including trumpets, four horns, and timpani: as large, therefore, as the great C minor piano concerto, K. 491. It lacks only the clarinets of Idomeneo's scena, Nos. 30 and 31, which follows immediately.

Elettra's outburst, especially in its fullest form, represents an exorcism. She symbolises disruption: violent, evil emotions like jealousy, revenge and anger. Elettra would rather see Idamante die than marry Ilia, just as the Queen of Night would allow Monostatos to marry her daughter to win his allegiance and defeat Sarastro.

Example 12.1

Elettra embodies the forces of irrationality, of immoderate emotions, which oppose the spirit of Enlightenment and which militate against reconciliation – the governing theme of this, as of other Mozart operas. Thus she carries immense symbolic weight, not only as a foil to Ilia but in opposition to the whole society of the opera, including the ultimately merciful divine order.

Ilia is the symbol of reconciliation. Initially torn between the affections of her heart and loyalty to her family, she finds by Act II that Crete has become a homeland, and in Act III, although it takes his sudden apparition and the threat of his death to unlock her tongue to her lover (if we discount the tedious equivocation of the added R. 10b), she aligns herself with the family of her enemy and tries to save Idamante's life. But the reconciliation of terrestrial enemies is only the foreground to the reconciliation of human and divine orders. Neptune's position is clear: a vow has been made and must be fulfilled. He is, therefore, a pagan version of the Old Testament god in his dealings with Jephtha until, affected by the renunciation of the struggle by Ilia, a leading representative of the defeated Trojans, he pronounces a lesser punishment for Idomeneo (the loss of his kingdom) which does not affect the innocent; indeed, it elevates them. Would that Jephtha's god had displayed such compassion.

The music of reconciliation is found in its purest form in the final scene: for Idomeneo's recitative of abdication Mozart found a serenity quite different from but matching that of Gluck's Orpheus. In 'Popoli, a voi l'ultima legge' he even found a new sonority, an ensemble in which the only wind instruments are clarinets and horns; the former, in particular, have not previously appeared without other members of the woodwind family. He also begins with strict imitation, at the unison and octave. There has, of course, been some imitative counterpoint earlier in the opera, but it is either the natural consequence of writing for two voices, or it is of a symphonic nature.[10] The strict imitation which opens No. 30 is just sufficient, in its clarity of exposition, to recall the techniques of sacred rather than theatrical music.

In this recitative, too, Mozart saturates the texture motivically. In the introduction, whose material he uses over the first fifteen bars and to which he constantly returns (see Ex. 12.2a), the rising arpeggio is only remotely related to motive A (compare Ex.1.1), but motive C is used literally, its sequential pattern according with a resolving dominant to tonic progression (in contrast to its indeterminate harmonic position in other crucial places, such as the stream of dominant sevenths in the sacrifice scene, No. 27, bars 19–23). Other figures in No. 30 relate to the 'reconciliation' complex associated with Ilia, notably the turn on to the third degree (bracketed 'x' in Ex. 12.2a, bar 2) and the dotted cadence figure which Strauss seemingly found significant enough to develop (see Ex. 6.1) and which is similar to the overture's motive E and thus to the reconciliation music (see Exx. 1.4 and 10.1). When this formally patterned, rather than recitative-like, music moves to the dominant, a new figure features the crotchet syncopation

Example 12.2

characteristic of the reconciliation material in music of Ilia and Idamante (bracketed in Ex. 12.2b; compare Ex. 10.1). There is also a reference to the overture's closing motive D; no longer chromatically anguished, this gently articulates the descending E♭ major arpeggio (Ex. 12.2a: 'z', in bar 6) and is glowingly repeated by the clarinets (bars 7–8).

This motivic saturation may or may not be intentional; coming at the close of the drama, when the king hands his power, in an organic and divinely approved succession, to his son, it is certainly serendipitous. Just as in Wagner's *Parsifal*, where the motives cease in the final pages to turn in on themselves and become extended, potentially unending, Mozart finds a harmonious resolution for many of the elements which have permeated the score. In this achievement, not the least part of which is sustaining dramatic intensity when all difficulties are resolved and Elettra has stormed out, Mozart reveals the inner essence of the genre to which *Idomeneo* must be assigned: *dramma per musica*, music drama.

Notes

1 Synopsis

1 I am grateful to Alan Bullock for help with the translation.

2 The *argomento* is confusing here, in omitting to mention Ilia's unwillingness to admit her love for Idamante.

3 The allusion is presumably to Varesco's immediate source, the *tragédie lyrique* by Danchet (see chapter 5).

4 French overture style normally belongs in slow introductions (see Ratner, *Classic Music*, p. 20). Similarities in *Idomeneo* include the long dotted values (this need not imply the gratuitous double dots and additional rests of Harnoncourt's Teldec recording of 1980).

5 Motive C is sometimes regarded as a motto or leitmotif representing Idamante. See chapter 10, p. 132.

6 I use 'Sturm und Drang' conventionally in musical, rather than literary, terms; see Ratner, *Classic Music*, p. 21.

7 Not to 'resolve' significant material in the tonic is exceptional, but not unique. Mozart normally observes decorum even in overtures, sometimes by unusual means (the monothematicism of *Die Zauberflöte*; the reversed recapitulation of *La clemenza di Tito*).

8 Dent, *Mozart's Operas* (2nd edn, p. 47) includes this 'second subject' among things which 'prepare us for tragedy'. Heartz refers to a passage from A major through A minor to C in the duet, No. 20a, written before the overture; thus the listener hears 'what sounds like an image of Ilia's constancy and faithfulness already in the overture' (*Mozart's Operas*, p. 49). More concretely, the move to C anticipates the melodic contour of No. 19, Ilia's 'Zeffiretti lusinghieri'.

9 Motive F reproduces R. 1, bar 36 almost exactly.

10 The direction is taken from the libretto. Heartz ('"Attaca subito"') points out that the direction appears at bar 36 in the autograph; all other scores give it at the end of the chorus, allowing only nine bars before Idomeneo lands.

11 If motive C is understood as an 'Idamante motive', this reference to the future victim is a particularly delicate irony. It appears in a passage of no fewer than sixteen bars which interrupt what is, in the libretto, a single line of recitative.

12 The sharp dotted figures from bar 24 resemble those in R. 2 (see Ex. 1.7). *MW* maintains simple recitative throughout; *NMA* indicates orchestra from bar 24 to the end. The autograph, followed by *NMA*,

indicates twenty bars of cut, covering the explanation of the vow; the Munich performing score cuts only eleven bars. The lines remain in Libretto 2. (This and all subsequent details concerning the cuts are from Münster, 'Neues zum Münchner *Idomeneo*; see also chapter 2.)

13 In R. 7, *MW* contains seventy-six bars; *NMA*, following cuts in the autograph and performing score, has fifty-eight. See chapter 2, p. 34 below.

14 Floros ('Das "Programm" in Mozarts Meisterouvertüren') relates bar 28 to motive C. The shape is not really very similar, but the *sf* and repeated note after a falling scale are common to both.

15 The Gavotte is 'hypothetically' inserted here by *NMA* (see Heartz, 'Vorwort', p. XVII), but is probably intended to follow Act III.

16 The ironic divertissement derives from French tradition; a comparable example is in Rameau's *Hippolyte et Aricie* Act III. Theseus, returned from Hades, finds hell at home (compare 'Fuor del mar, ho un mar in seno', No. 12 of *Idomeneo*); he is forced to ask Neptune to destroy his son. In Gluck's *Iphigénie en Aulide*, Act I, the divertissement celebrates the arrival of Iphigenia, destroying Agamemnon's hopes of saving her from sacrifice.

17 A large cut is prescribed (*NMA* has thirty-four bars against sixty-four in *MW*), eliminating much explanation, including (again) the vow; the words remained in Libretto 2.

18 Mozart set part of the recitative and aria as the soprano concert aria with piano obbligato 'Ch'io mi scordi di te?' (K. 505). The authorship of the words is unknown; Mozart is more likely to have turned to a Vienna poet (perhaps da Ponte) than back to Varesco.

19 Speeches cut (reading of *NMA*) include mention of Ilia's parents and the sack of Troy. Münster ('Münchner *Idomeneo*') suggests that the cut was in reality shorter, retaining a mention of Idamante picked up by Idomeneo in R. 12.

20 David Cairns, *Responses*, p. 61, and Janos Liebner, *Mozart on the Stage*, pp. 52–3. See also Rushton, 'La vittima è Idamante'.

21 This dialogue is cut in *NMA*, implying its omission in 1781; but it is in the libretto and survives in the Munich score.

22 The voice parts were revised in 1786 to accommodate the tenor Idamante: *NMA* superimposes both versions.

23 Mozart insisted on recitative here rather than an aria. See chapter 2, p. 31, below.

24 The libretto explains No. 18 thus: 'The tempest continues. The Cretans fly in terror, and by singing the following chorus, and with pantomime, express all their terror, all of which forms an analogous action, and closes the act as the only divertissement.'

25 For a positive evaluation of the 1786 Duet, see Heartz, 'Mozart's Tragic Muse'.

26 See also Heartz, 'The Great Quartet in Mozart's *Idomeneo*'. Marita McClymonds has pointed out that such quartets occurred quite frequently in *opera seria* (paper read at the 1991 Royal Musical Association conference on Mozart). *MW* lacks the tenor version. Singing the castrato line an octave down (as on Schmidt-Isserstedt's 1972

recording) makes the texture absurdly gruff (e.g. bars 39, 97). Mozart used the original pitch, high for a tenor (e.g. bars 39 ff. or 93), or recomposed the top three parts. Perhaps to accommodate the Vienna singers, Elettra receives more of the top line; from bar 60, to preserve imitation in the same octave, Idamante's line is passed to Ilia and Ilia's to Elettra (such changes in ensemble passages do not affect the association of music with text).

27   The whole scene was omitted in 1781.

28   Floros ('Das "Programm" in Mozart's Meisterouvertüren') detects motive C in bar 6, but while the allusion to Idamante's sacrifice is clear, if indirect, the musical shape is markedly different.

29   See Rushton, 'A Reconciliation Motive in Idomeneo?'

30   In 1781 No. 24 was reduced to a single section and No. 26 to half its original length; both cuts seriously reduce the impact of these ritual movements. Heartz (*Mozart's Operas*, p. 30) provides further arguments against them.

31   No. 27 was intended for omission in 1781, but there is evidence of its restoration. It was not included in 1786. The *NMA* bar numbers are continuous before and after the aria's original location.

32   The following dialogue was much reduced in 1781. *NMA* is shorter than *MW* by forty bars; as with all Mozart's cuts in Act III, this accelerates the action at the expense of some fine dramatic music.

33   On the four versions of the subterranean voice, see Table 2.1. (p. 42).

34   The original recitative (*MW* appendix, 355; *NMA* p. 569) makes this the most imposing solo scene of the opera. Mozart substituted a shorter version (*NMA* main text, 474; *MW* appendix, 359) which ends in D minor, and is thus incompatible with the C minor aria

35   See chapter 2, and Heartz, 'Raaff's Last Aria'.

36   *Tragédie lyrique* integrated ballet fully into its structure. In concluding thus *Idomeneo* may seem to be conforming to the origins of its libretto, and to the Gluck model; but in wealthy centres, particularly courts, *opera seria* was also conventionally followed by a ballet, not necessarily by the same composer or in any way integrated with the opera itself. In his letter of 30 December 1781 Mozart expressed particular pleasure at being allowed to compose the ballet himself.

2   Genesis of an operone

1   The ducat was not, at this period, in a consistent relationship with the more standard gulden (or florin); calculations here are based on the ordinary (as opposed to the imperial or Kremnitz) ducat, using the values itemised by Dexter Edge, 'Mozart's Fee for *Così fan tutte*', *Journal of the Royal Musical Association* 116 (1991), 211–35. Edge's article also provides the information drawn on here regarding fees paid at the Viennese court opera.

2   For a discussion of the libretto and its relationship to the sources see chapter 5; see also Kurt Kramer, 'Das Libretto zu Mozarts *Idomeneo*: Quellen und Umgestaltung der Fabel'.

3 No detailed analysis of the paper-types used in *Idomeneo* has yet been published. Work towards such an analysis has been done by Dr Alan Tyson, to whom I am indebted for all material on paper-types in this chapter.

4 For a full account of the rediscovered Munich material see Robert Münster, 'Neues zum Münchner *Idomeneo*'.

5 In the old complete edition, both authentic versions of the recitative are relegated to the appendix; the main text gives a compromise version, consisting of the shorter recitative without its last six bars, which are replaced by the last three of the longer version (personal communication from Daniel Heartz). This shocking editorial confection was the most familiar version until the adoption of the *NMA* text. The editor presumably thought the original recitative too long but was unwilling to forgo the aria.

6 See note 4, above.

7 The sources for the versions of the oracle's speech are discussed by Heartz in *NMA* Vorwort, p. xiv.

8 The circumstances surrounding the first performances are discussed by Münster, 'Neues zum Münchner *Idomeneo*'.

9 See Nerina Medici di Marignano and Rosemary Hughes, eds., *A Mozart Pilgrimage: Being the Travel Diaries of Vincent & Mary Novello in the Year 1829* (London, 1955), 114–15.

10 *Pfeffer und Salz* I, pp. 15–17; reprinted in O. E. Deutsch: *Mozart: die Dokumente seines Lebens* (Kassel, Basle, London, and New York, 1961), 236 (translated as *Mozart: A Documentary Biography*, p. 270). The event is also referred to in H. A. O. Reichard: *Taschenbuch für die Schaubühne auf das Jahr 1787* (Gotha, 1786), in a note on recent performances in private Viennese theatres; see C. Eisen: *New Mozart Documents* (London, 1991), no. 70.

11 A sketch sheet of Mozart's in the Deutsche Staatsbibliothek, Berlin, is reproduced by Ulrich Konrad ('Mozart's Sketches', *Early Music* 20 (1992), 119–30; see p. 123). It includes twenty-one bars of duet material, untexted, in A major, written on two staves in the soprano and tenor clefs, and it is dated without explanation '*c.* 1785–6' by Konrad; the paper, according to Tyson (personal communication), is indeed one used in late 1785 and early 1786. Konrad suggests that it may have been intended for a duet in *Der Schauspieldirektor*, and at this date it could also have been intended for *Figaro*. Neither work, however, calls for a soprano–tenor duet, and nor does any other work of the period except, arguably, *Idomeneo*. The sketch has clear points of resemblance with K. 489, although the metric structure does not accord well with the text Mozart eventually used (he often, however, drafted music *before* the text for it was written).

12 Mozart is known to have used the term 'operone' only once, in his last letter (14 October 1791), referring to Salieri's and Cavalieri's reactions to *Die Zauberflöte*; it seems an apt word, re-exchanging Italian and German, for the work Mozart himself described as a 'grosse Opera'.

3 'Madame Dorothea Wendling is arcicontentissima': the performers of *Idomeneo*

1 An early attempt to sketch the significance of Mozart's singers in *Idomeneo* is by Ernst Lewicki, 'Die Stimmcharaktere im *Idomeneo*'; *Bericht über die musikwissenschaftliche Tagung der Internationalen Stiftung Mozarteum in Salzburg, vom 2. bis 5. August 1931*, ed. Erich Schenk (Leipzig: Breitkopf and Härtel, 1932), 158–60.

2 For a summary of Raaff's earlier career, see Pierluigi Petrobelli, 'The Italian Years of Anton Raaff', *Mozart-Jahrbuch 1973–4*, pp. 233–73.

3 'His [Johann Baptist Wendling's] wife has been singled out as one of our best dramatic singers [Theatersängerinnen]' (Christian Friedrich Daniel Schubart, *Ideen zu einer Ästhetik der Tonkunst* (Vienna: Degen, 1806; reprint, with introduction and index by Fritz and Margrit Kaiser, Hildesheim: Olms, 1969) 144). In his *Hildegard von Hohenthal*, partly a novel and partly a treatise on aesthetics and technical musical matters as well as a commentary on contemporary opera, Wilhelm Heinse described Dorothea as the star of Mannheim's golden age (Heinse, *Hildegard von Hohenthal*, 2 vols., in: *Sämmtliche Werke VI–VII* (Leipzig: Insel, 1903), I: 171–2). See also Hans Müller, 'Wilhelm Heinse als Musikschriftsteller', *Vierteljahrsschrift für Musikwissenschaft* 3 (1887), 585–6.

4 Wieland wrote to Sophie de la Roche on 24 December 1777 that the hours he had spent working with Dorothea Wendling were some of the most agreeable he had ever spent (Hans Werner Seiffert, ed., *Briefe der Weimarer Zeit* (21. September 1772–31. Dezember 1777), *Wielands Briefwechsel V* (Berlin: Akademie-Verlag, 1983), 693; Thomas C. Starnes, *Christoph Martin Wieland: Leben und Werk aus zeitgenössischen Quellen chronologisch dargestellt*, 3 vols. (Sigmaringen: Thobecke, 1987), I: 627). Mozart (letter of 13 November 1780) heard Mara in Munich and was less than impressed.

5 Arthur Schuring, ed., *Leopold Mozart: Reiseaufzeichnungen 1763–1771: 27 faksimilierte handschriftliche Blätter* (Dresden: Laube, 1920), 65.

6 Roland Würtz, 'Wendling', *The New Grove Dictionary of Music and Musicians*, ed. Stanley Sadie (London: Macmillan, 1980), XX: 339–40.

7 Charles Burney, *The Present State of Music in Germany, The Netherlands, and the United Provinces or The Journal of a Tour through those Countries, Undertaken to Collect Materials for A General History of Music*, 2 vols. (London: Becket, Robson and Robinson, 1773), I: 93.

8 Hans Schmid, 'Zur Biographie des bayerischen Hofsängers Giovanni Valesi (Walleshauser)', *Musik in Bayern: Halbjahresschrift der Gesellschaft für bayerische Musikgeschichte* 10 (1975), 28–30.

9 Letter of 14 November 1777. Einstein (in the third edition of Köchel's catalogue) believed that Mozart wrote the *scena* and aria 'Ma che vi fece' – 'Sperai vicino il lido' (K. 368) for her. This claim is treated with a degree of caution by Stefan Kunze, ed., *NMA* II: 7/2 (*Arien, Szenen, Ensembles und Chöre mit Orchester* II), xvii.

10 Robert Münster, 'W. A. Mozarts "Bernreider" Kanon', *Mozart–Jahrbuch 1962–3*, 182; and 'Mozart . . . "Beym Herzoge Clemens . . ."', *Mozart–Jahrbuch 1965–6*, 139.

11 The works are the two French ariettes K. 284d and 295b.
12 Leopold Mozart, *Reiseaufzeichnungen*, p. 12.
13 The differences between the two are characterised by their own compositions; Cannabich's symphonies and ballet music contrast strongly with Wendling's concerto output.
14 The most exhaustive study of Raaff's career is still Heinz Freiberger, *Anton Raaff (1714–1797): sein Leben und Wirken als Beitrag zur Musikgeschichte des 18. Jahrhunderts* (Hoffnungsthal and Cologne: Pilgram, 1929).
15 There is some uncertainty about which concert Mozart was referring to. 'Non so d'onde viene' is expressly mentioned in the programme for the 'Concert spirituel' of 18 June, but that is later than Mozart's letter. The concert of 28 May is the last in the series in which Raaff had been participating since 13 April (Constant Pierre, *Histoire du Concert spirituel 1725–1790*, Publications de la Société Française de Musicologie 3: 3 (Paris: Heugel, 1975), 308–9). A review in the *Journal de Paris* of 15 April makes it clear that enthusiasm for Raaff's performances was widespread (cited *ibidem*, p. 192).
    At least two versions of J. C. Bach's setting are known: (1) the version from *Alessandro nell'Indie*, premiered at the Teatro di San Carlo, Naples on 20 January 1762 in which Raaff took the title role and (2) the version from the pasticcio *Ezio*, first produced at the King's Theatre, London on 24 November 1764, almost certainly heard there by Mozart (letter of 8 February 1765; later that year he also wrote a substitute aria for it: 'Va, dal furor portata' K. 19c). The two versions (published respectively in facsimile in Ernest Warburton, ed., *Alessandro nell'Indie: Opera Seria in Three Acts, Libretto after Metastasio, The Collected Works of Johann Christian Bach, 1735–1782* (New York and London: Garland, 1985), III: fols. 23r–25v and Ernest Warburton, ed., '*La clemenza di Scipione and Music from London Pasticci*, The Collected Works of Johann Christian Bach, 1735–1782 (New York and London: Garland, 1990), IX: 103–17) differ in their middle sections, and the text is different. For a study of the relationships between all four settings see Stefan Kunze, 'Die Vertonungen der Arie 'Non sò d'onde viene' von J. Chr. Bach und W. A. Mozart,' *Analecta musicologica* 2 (1965), 85–111.
16 Bauer and Deutsch, II: 377: 'Er marht mir zu viell [*sic*] ins Cantabile.'
17 *NMA* II: 7/2 (see note 9 above), 59–76.
18 Heartz, 'Raaff's Last Aria', pp. 534–9.
19 The history of these changes is laid out *ibidem*, pp. 520–9. See also chapter 2, pp. 32 and 36 above.
20 Facsimile in Heartz, 'Raaff's Last Aria', pp. 526, 528, 531 and 532.
21 *NMA*, p. xi.
22 *NMA* II: 7/2, 77–84.
23 See Robert Münster, 'Das Münchener *Idomeneo*–Orchester von 1781', *Bayerische Staatsbibliothek*, pp. 106–21.
24 That such a combination was typical for a *symphonie concertante* is made clear by Robert D. Levin, *Who Wrote the Mozart Four-Wind Concertante?* (Stuyvesant, N.Y.: Pendragon, 1988), 126; on Cambini, see p. 9.

25 Levin, *Who Wrote the Mozart Four-Wind Concertante?* pp. 138–54.
26 See also Angus Heriot, *The Castrati in Opera* (London: Secker and Warburg, 1956), 120–1; Otto Michtner, *Das alte Burgtheater als Opernbühne von der Einführung des deutschen Singspiels* (1778) *bis zum Tod Kaiser Leopolds II. (1792)*, Theatergeschichte Österreichs III: 1 (Vienna: Bohlhaus, 1970), 379 and note 20.
27 Ceccarelli had come to Salzburg just after Mozart left in October 1777. By the time Mozart returned home, he was a good friend of the family, and to judge from the comments Mozart made to his father from Munich, became a good friend of Mozart's as well; he was in Vienna with Mozart after Archbishop Colloredo had moved there in early 1781 (letter of 17 March 1781).
28 Felix Joseph Lipowsky, *Baierisches Musik-Lexikon* (Munich: Giel, 1811; reprint, Hildesheim and New York: Olms, 1982), 253–5.
29 Taddeo Wiel, *I teatri musicali veneziani del settecento: catalogo delle opere in musica rappresentate nel secolo xviii in Venezia (1701–1800)* (Venice: Visentini, 1897; reprinted Leipzig: Peters, 1979), 293–4. I am grateful to Robert Münster for this reference.
30 Petrobelli, 'Italian Years of Anton Raaff', p. 270; John Rosselli, 'The Castrati as a Professional Group and a Social Phenomenon, 1550–1850', *Acta musicologica* 60 (1988), 172, note 108.
31 Margret Dietrich has proposed Adamberger for the High Priest on the specious grounds that he was of a pupil of Valesi, possibly the 1781 Munich High Priest (see chapter 2, p. 41, above). Dietrich favours Lange as Ilia and Bernasconi as Elettra (Margret Dietrich, '"Wiener Fassungen" des *Idomeneo*', *Mozart–Jahrbuch 1973–4*, p. 65).
32 For a summary of what is known about Countess Thun, see Alfred Orel, 'Gräfin Wilhelmine Thun (Mäzenatentum in Wiens klassischer Zeit)', *Mozart–Jahrbuch 1956*, pp. 89–101.
33 See Deutsch, *Mozart: A Documentary Biography*, p. 267; Heinrich August Ottokar Reichard, *Taschenbuch für die Schaubühne auf das Jahr 1797* (Gotha, [1786]), 94–5; Eisen, *New Mozart Documents* (London, 1991), 44, document 70; I am grateful to Professor Eisen for sharing the contents of this with me prior to publication. The other three private theatres belonged to Count Altheim, Count Johann Esterhazy, and Herr Lackenbauer.
34 Deutsch, *Mozart: A Documentary Biography*, p. 270.
35 See Ernst Franz Schmid, 'August Clemens Graf Hatzfeld', *Mozart–Jahrbuch 1954*, 14–32.
36 Dietrich, '"Wiener Fassungen" des *Idomeneo*', 57.

4 The genre of *Idomeneo*

1 Probably written by the librettist Calzabigi, the dedication of *Alceste* is available in English in H. and E. H. Mueller von Asow, *The Collected Correspondence and Papers of Christoph Willibald Gluck* (London: Barrie and Rockliff, 1962), p. 22.
2 Mozart, *Verzeichnüss aller meiner Werke*, Mozart's *Thematic Catalogue, A facsimile, British Library, Stefan Zweig MS63*, introduction and

transcription by Albi Rosenthal and Alan Tyson, London: The British Library, 1991, entry for 5 September 1791. Mozart writes 'opera seria . . . ridotta á vera opera dal Sigre Mazzolà . . .' The changes include the insertion of several ensembles and a concerted finale. Heartz observes that '*Idomeneo* is not an opera seria and was never so called . . . unlike *Tito*' ('The Invention of *Idomeneo*', p. 36). See also Heartz, 'Mozart and his Italian contemporaries'.

3 See Deutsch, *Mozart: A Documentary Biography*, pp. 95–100.

4 Jommelli's *Armida* is in the facsimile series 'Italian Opera 1640–1770' (New York: Garland, 1983).

5 Francesco Algarotti, *Saggio sopra l'opera in musica* (1755), containing a complete libretto in French based on Racine's *Iphigénie*.

6 Jommelli worked with a librettist, Verazi, beside whom Varesco appears timid, at Rome, Stuttgart, Mannheim, and Naples (*Ifigenia in Tauride*, 1771). See Marita McClymonds, 'Mattia Verazi and the Opera at Mannheim, Stuttgart, and Ludwigsburg', *Studies in Music* (University of Western Ontario) 7/2 (1982), 99–136.

7 Coltellini was also a reforming librettist, who worked with Gluck (*Telemaco*) as well as Traetta. Mozart set his *opera buffa La finta semplice* in 1768.

8 *Orfeo ed Euridice* (1762) is an *azione teatrale* rather than a reform of *opera seria*, but in style it is as radical a departure from its tradition as *Alceste*. More typical is Mozart's *festa teatrale Ascanio in Alba* (1771), written for the wedding of an Austrian archduke.

9 The alleged influence of *Alceste* on *Idomeneo* is considered by Platoff ('Writing about Influences'), who refers to earlier discussions of this question.

10 Jahn, *The Life of Mozart* II, p. 163. Curiously, Jahn states that both scenes use trombones; but they are used only in the *Alceste* scene.

11 Floros, 'Das "Programm" in Mozarts Meisterouvertüren', p. 149.

12 *Günther von Schwarzburg* is published in *Denkmaler deutscher Tonkunst VIII/IX* (1902, reprinted 1957).

13 Roland Würtz: 'Ignaz Holzbauer und das Teutsche', *Studies in Music* (University of Western Ontario) 7 (1982), 89–98. Würtz concentrates on the connection between Holzbauer's opera and *Die Zauberflöte* because of their German libretti, but in structure and nobility of tone *Idomeneo* is a much closer parallel. On Mannheim and Munich see also Eugene K. Wolf, 'The Mannheim Court'.

14 Respectively pp. 240 and 200 of the score, see note 12, above.

15 Letter of 11 September 1778; 'his' refers to Piccinni's supporter Baron Grimm. The Piccinnist nature of *Idomeneo* was noticed by Eric Blom (*Stepchildren of Music*, London 1925, p. 63–4). Saint Foix's suggestion (*W.A. Mozart* III: 231) that the opening of the *Idomeneo* quartet derives from the overture to *Roland* fails the test of singularity: given that both use a dotted rhythm and a descending arpeggio they could hardly be more different.

  Shortly before *Idomeneo*, Piccinni worked on another adaptation of an old French libretto, *Atys*, which culminates in a long quartet with textural similarities to Mozart's, and has the same key-signature, though Piccinni's is in C minor, not E♭. *Atys* was probably published in 1780; Mozart might conceivably have seen a score.

16 Saint Foix (*W. A. Mozart* III: 230) claims that not only procedures but even themes in Arbace's 'Sventurata Sidon' are taken from *Ariadne*.

5 From myth to libretto

1 Judges 11, 30–6.

2 A historic opinion formulated by Racine in the preface to *Iphigénie*. Later works based on *Jephtha* include a fiancé, as Idamante has Ilia and Iphigenia Achilles; and they also tend towards a happy ending. An exception to the stage ban was Pellegrin and Montéclair's *Jephté* (Paris Opera, 1732). This was certainly influenced by the Danchet–Campra *Idoménée*, notably in the delayed recognition of father and child; to this end Pellegrin has Jephtha exiled for ten years, the traditional length of the Trojan War. Girdlestone, *La Tragédie en musique*, 259ff.

3 Pausanias, *Description of Greece* V.25.9. For a modern view of Idomeneus, see Michael Wood, *In Search of the Trojan War* (London: BBC, 1985). For an extended discussion of the origins of the story see R. Angermüller, 'Bemerkungen zum Idomeneus-Stoff', *Mozart-Jahrbuch 1973–4*.

4 Hyginus, *Fabulae* 81; Homer, *Iliad* XIII and *Odyssey* III; Apollodorus, *Epitome* VI; Lycophron, *Alexandra*.

5 H. J. Rose classifies the story among 'Märchen' (fairytales), according it only five lines in *A Handbook of Greek Mythology* (London 1928, often reprinted), p. 291.

6 Virgil, *Aeneid* III, 121; Rose, *A Handbook of Greek Mythology* cites Servius, *Commentary on Virgil* III.121; Pausanias IX.33.4; and Pseudo-Plutarch, *De fluviis*, IX.1.

7 Leopold's letter from Paris, 16 May 1766; Wolfgang's from Bologna, 8 September 1770. He tells his sister that he has reached the second part; it is not known if he reached the sections pertaining to Idomeneus.

8 The mad slaughter of a beloved person had appeared in an earlier *tragédie lyrique*, Quinault and Lully's *Atys*.

9 See R. Angermüller, '*Idomeneo* auf der Opern- und Schauspielbühne des 18. und frühen 19. Jahrhunderts', in *Bayerische Staatsbibliothek: W. A. Mozart, 'Idomeneo' 1781–1981*, pp. 44–61. Algarotti's *Iphigenia* libretto (see chapter 4, note 6) was anticipated by Mattia Verazi in *Ifigenia in Aulide*, set by Jommelli (Rome, Mannheim, and elsewhere, from 1751).

10 Crébillon's tragedy was probably the first stage work on the subject.

11 Iliona is mentioned in Virgil (*Aeneid* I.653) as Priam's eldest daughter; the Trojans offer her sceptre to Dido, an incident reproduced by Berlioz (*Les Troyens*, Act III).

12 Dent (*Mozart's Operas*, p. 66), a victim of fashionable anticlericalism, had already observed (*ibidem*, p. 62): 'Priests in opera are always odious.' Did he think the High Priest had 'stage-managed' the storm and the monster?

13 Girdlestone, *La Tragédie en musique*, pp. 201–7. Girdlestone deals even more extensively with seventeenth- and eighteenth-century renditions of the Idomeneus myth in '*Idomenée . . . Idomeneo*: Transformations d'un thème 1699–1781', *Recherches sur la musique française classique* 13 (1973), 102–32.

14 Pietro Metastasio, 'Estratto dell'arte poetica d'Aristotele e considerazioni su la medesima', in *Tutte le opere*, ed. B. Brunelli Bonetti (5 vols., Verona, 1951–65; *Opera varie* 2), II: 973.

15 A reference to the theatre intendant Count Seeau and the claim that 'alles nach der Vorschrift gemacht worden' (all has been done as commanded) are to be found in Leopold Mozart's letter of 11 November 1780. Leopold also mentions the 'vorgeschriebenen Plan' (prescribed layout) on 18 November.

16 Dent, *Mozart's Operas* (1947), 34.

17 For Idomenée, discord betwen his royal house and the gods Poseidon/Neptune and Aphrodite/Venus dates back to his alleged grandparents Minos and Pasiphae. A full description of the myth and a citation of sources appear under 'Pasiphae' in Pierre Grimal, *Dictionnaire de la mythologie grecque et romaine* (Paris, 1951), trans. by A. R. Maxwell Hyslop as *The Dictionary of Classical Mythology* (Oxford, 1985), 348 and 502.

18 The progressive psychological unfolding evident in Ilia's first aria is discussed in Hocquard, *Idomenée*, pp. 59–63, and in chapter 8, p. 109, below.

19 Dent, *Mozart's Operas* (1947), 45.

20 Letter of 6 December 1783.

6 *Idomeneo* after Mozart

1 Deutsch, *Mozart: A Documentary Biography*, pp. 199, 213–14; see also chapters 2 and 3, above.

2 The libretto was arranged by G. F. Treitschke, who later worked on Beethoven's *Fidelio*.

3 On Mozart's publishers, see W. Rehm in Landon, *The Mozart Compendium*, pp. 423–4, and L. von Köchel: *Chronologisch-thematisches Verzeichnis sämtlicher Tonwerke Wolfgang Amade Mozarts* (6th edn. by F. Giegling, A. Weinmann, and G. Sievers, Leipzig, 1964).

4 Loewenberg, *Annals of Opera* (2nd edn revised, London, 1965, col 386) lists a performance in Italian at Budapest (1803); otherwise, most performances were in German, involving at least four German translators.

5 The score is lost; these details derive from the printed libretto (Bibliothèque nationale, Paris). See also R. Angermüller, 'Eine französische *Idomeneo*-Bearbeitung aus dem Jahre 1822. Ein Beitrag zu Mozart-Bearbeitungen im 19. Jahrhundert in Frankreich', in *Mitteilungen der Internationalen Stiftung Mozarteum Salzburg*, 21 (1973).

6 Loewenberg, *Annals of Opera*, says *Idomeneo* music was used in a French pastiche in 1825, and in Paris concert performances in 1846 (extracts) and 1902.

7   Otto Jahn, *W. A. Mozart* (Leipzig, 1856), trans. as *The Life of Mozart* (London, 1882; 3 vols).
8   *Berlinische musikalische Zeitung* 2 (1806), 11–12.
9   *Mozarts Opern: kritische Erläuterungen* (Leipzig, 1848).
10 Jahn, *W. A. Mozart*, pp. 148, 145, 156. This nationalistic tendency – Jahn wrote in the period before the unification of Germany – was excised by Hermann Abert in his revision of Jahn. Generally better versed in Italian opera, Abert makes several references to specific models and to the strength of Italian taste in Munich. H. Abert: *W. A. Mozart. Neubearbeitete und erweiterte Ausgabe von Otto Jahns Mozart* I (Leipzig, 1923), from p. 839.
11 *Aus dem Opernleben der Gegenwart* (Berlin, 1884), reprinted in *The Collected Musical Criticism of Eduard Hanslick* (Farnborough, 1971), III: 107–14.
12 A. Heuss, 'Mozarts *Idomeneo* als Quelle für *Don Giovanni* und *Die Zauberflöte*', *Zeitschrift für Musikwissenschaft* 13 (1931), 177–99.
13 A monster similarly visible as consisting only of a head featured in Colin Graham's production for the Aldeburgh Festival *c.* 1970.
14 See J. Rice, *W. A. Mozart: 'La clemenza di Tito'* (Cambridge, 1991) for the reception history of that opera.
15 E. Lert, *Mozart auf dem Theater*, from page 293.
16 For details see R. Angermüller, 'Bemerkungen zum *Idomeneus*-Stoff', pp. 293–7.
17 Loewenberg lists one sung in Italian, at Basle, that year.
18 Wolf-Ferrari's version formed the basis of one of the earliest 'complete' recordings, confined to two LPs (Mercury MG 10053).
19 Wilhelm Zentner, in *Neue Zeitschrift für Musik* 98 (1931), 622–3 (and not p. 621 as in the periodical's index).
20 H. G. Bunte, in *Neue Zeitschrift für Musik* 98 (1931), 329.
21 E. Blom, *Mozart* (London, 1935), 99, 279–82.
22 A. A. Abert, 'The Operas of Mozart', pp. 134–5. Abert's account is otherwise unexceptionable.
23 E. J. Dent, 'Idomeneo', *The Listener*, 26 February 1948.
24 Rice, *W. A. Mozart: 'La clemenza di Tito'*.
25 The version of 'Fuor del mar' sung by Richard Lewis is some thirty bars shorter than the 1786 version (though, perversely, he supplies a cadenza); yet it appears to be cut from the 1781 version until the 1786 lead-in to the following scene. The economical reissue of this recording (EMI, CHS 7 63685 2) cannot offset its lack of dramatic continuity and generally slow tempi.
26 *The Musical Times* 124 (1983), 440–1.
27 EMI IC 191–29 271 (1972), not available on CD.
28 On three CDs, DGG 429 864–2.
29 Respectively on Nikolaus Harnoncourt's recording (1980: TELDEC 8. 35547) and John Elliot Gardiner's (1991: DGG ARCHIV 431674–2) (each 3 CDs).
30 Both Lewis (note 25) and Pavarotti (1983, Decca 411–805–2) were working under John Pritchard in association with Glyndebourne; the 1983 version, significantly as a sign of the times, is virtually complete (3 CDs).

31 Davis's recordings for Philips (both on 3 CDs) are (1968) 420 130–2, and (1991) 422 537–2.

32 Not quite all the music available is included; see my review in *Early Music*, November 1991.

33 L. von Köchel, *Chronologisch-thematisches Verzeichnis sämtlicher Tonwerke Wolfgang Amadé Mozarts*, 3rd edn, revised by A. Einstein (Leipzig, 1937), 445.

34 Letter from Strauss to Bruno von Niessen, 27 February 1932, in *Der Strom der Töne trug mich fort*, ed. F. Grasberger (Tutzing 1967), 338.

35 'Richard Strauss's *Elektra*', interview with the composer in *Allgemeine Musik-Zeitung* 39, 25 September 1908, p. 669.

36 *Idomeneo*, revised by L. Wallerstein and R. Strauss (Magdeburg 1931). For a detailed description of Strauss's alterations see S. Kohler, 'Die *Idomeneo*-Bearbeitung von Lothar Wallerstein und Richard Strauss', in *Bayerische Staatsbibliothek*, p. 176. On the soprano notation of K. 490 in Mozart's autograph, see p. 45.

37 Letter from Strauss to von Niessen, 27 February 1932, in *Der Strom der Töne*, 338.

38 Review by 'Hamel' of the Berlin performance in a newspaper cutting held by the Richard Strauss Institute, Munich, and identified as 'D A Z. 13/11 32'. The precise source is unknown to me.

39 'P. Zsch.', writing in the *Dresdner Nachrichten*, 15 November 1932.

40 Review of the Magdeburg première in a newspaper cutting held by the Richard Strauss Institute and identified as 'BBZ 27/4 31' (presumably *Berliner Börsen Zeitung*, which employed Köppen in the 1930s). See, however, the favourable review by Viktor Junk, *Neue Zeitschrift für Musik* 98 (1931), 410–11.

41 Letter of 11 April 1932, in *Richard Strauss: Autographen in München und Wien. Verzeichnis*, ed. G. Brosche and K. Dachs (Tutzing 1979), 368.

42 Letter from Strauss to von Niessen, 17 February 1932.

43 *Ibidem.*

44 R. Strauss, *Betrachtungen und Erinnerungen*, ed. W. Schuh (Munich 1989), 72.

7 General structure of *Idomeneo*

1 On Elettra's aria, see letter of 3 January 1781. As a result of including or omitting various numbers in Act III (22, 27, 29, 30a/31) widely divergent timings appear on recordings.

2 Daniel Heartz refers in particular to the obscurity of No. 13, 'Idol mio' (*Mozart's Operas*, p. 23).

3 Varesco is stiffer in his adherence to these line-lengths than Calzabigi in *Alceste*. For a fuller account of Italian libretto verse in the eighteenth century, see T. Carter, *W. A. Mozart: 'Le nozze di Figaro'* (Cambridge, 1987), 76–87. On versification, see also D. Kimbell, *Italian Opera* (Cambridge, 1991), xvii.

4 Mozart possibly regarded such combinations as AI, OI, IE, OE, and EO as hard to sing smoothly as elisions. IO is not difficult: perhaps the dignity of the deity ('Dio') required two syllables.

5   *Versi sdruccioli* particularly suit patter-singing (Carter, *W. A. Mozart: 'Le nozze di Figaro'*, p. 80), and Varesco may have avoided them for their association with *opera buffa* (he makes use of them in the unfinished *L'oca del Cairo*). He ignored one precedent within the immediate tradition; Jommelli apparently relished stanzas of variable length, for instance, nine and then three lines. See McClymonds, 'Mattia Verazi and the Opera', *Studies in Music* (1982), 100–1.

6   See the synopsis; C. Rosen, *Sonata Forms* (New York, 1980), chapter 4 ('Aria', particularly pp. 43–68); Hirschberg, 'Formal and Dramatic Aspects of Sonata Form in Mozart's *Idomeneo*', which deals mainly with structural proportion; and Webster, 'The Analysis of Mozart's Arias', 114–22.

7   Precise punctuation is not a feature of eighteenth-century librettos, still less of scores. I have used the punctuation of Libretto 2 except after verse 1/3 and verse 2/5, where it has a comma. Neither *MW* nor *NMA* places a full stop after 'affanni'.

8   This form of sonata, without development, is sometimes called 'slow-movement sonata form'; a perfect example is in Mozart's string Quartet K. 387. However, the tonal-thematic pattern also suits fast tempi, for example, the overture to *Le nozze di Figaro*.

9   The rearrangement of 'E' provides the performers with least extended ranges – the horn and voice – with effective, and in the former case playable, scales, though the second horn scale, f' to f", remains very difficult on the instrument of Mozart's day.

10 Tonal and verbal reprises do not quite coincide in Nos. 1 and 4, but the sense of return is unmistakable and exact coincidence is restored well before the point at which the exposition modulated (see chapters 8 and 11). This binary form differs more in expression than in underlying structure from the first type described.

11 The ternary sonata-aria is sometimes referred to as 'transformed Da Capo' (see H. Smither, *The Oratorio in the Classic Era* (Oxford, 1987), 78–82, and N. Temperley, *Haydn: The Creation* (Cambridge, 1991), 74). The crucial difference is that in true da capo arias, the first section ends in the tonic, not the dominant, and the reprise is a repeat, not a recomposition.

12 Stanley Sadie observed after hearing it that the aria is 'about as helpful to the drama as a tourniquet to the circulation' (*The Musical Times* 124 (1983), 440–1). For a more positive view see Heartz, *Mozart's Operas*, p. 58. The problem, however, is precisely that, in Heartz's phrase, No. 10b reflects 'one of the latest fashions in arias'.

13 It is perhaps no coincidence that this Weber-like form (unlike many others) was not interfered with in Wolf-Ferrari's version.

14 The lively and socially not elevated 3/8 metre even appears at the end of Act I in Jommelli's 'old-fashioned' *Armida*. The key of A major, incidentally, was much favoured for love duets in this period.

8   Two soliloquies

1   The incidence of G minor in Mozart's mature work is unusually high for a minor key. Other heroines, such as Konstanze in *Die Entführung* ('Traurigkeit') and Pamina in *Die Zauberflöte* ('Ach, ich fühl's'), use it at the nadir of their fortunes.

2   These include the Neapolitan sixth (bar 24), two diminished sevenths, and an augmented sixth on G (bar 25). See Rushton, ' . . . hier wird es besser seyn, ein blosses Recitativ zu machen'.

3   David Cairns regards bars 19–20 of 'Fuor del mar' as a version of motive C (*Responses*, p. 63).

4   Similar falling sevenths underline Leporello's terror in the graveyard (*Don Giovanni* No. 22, e.g. bars 24–6).

5   In the revision, the final cadence is elided with the following scene.

6   The only other aria with trumpets is No. 29; No. 4 has four horns.

7   See Ratner, *Classic Music*, for a discussion of topics, and W. J. Allanbrook, *Rhythmic Gesture in Mozart* (University of Chicago Press, 1983), for an exploration from this point of view of Mozart's comedies.

9   The musical language of *Idomeneo*

1   The 'tinta' or 'colorito' was identified by Basevi in 1859 as the sign of a unified conception within certain of Verdi's operas. See Julian Budden, *The Operas of Verdi* I (London, 1973), 40, and II (London, 1978), p. 53.

2   Referring to 'motive C', Dent said, 'there is no reason to call it a *leitmotiv* or give it a ridiculous name' (*Mozart's Operas*, 1st edn (London, 1913), 80; in the second edition (p. 50), 'ridiculous' is replaced by 'Wagnerian').

3   Consideration for dal Prato would not, of course, determine the key of the aria composed in 1786, still in B♭. It is certainly curious that this aria and the 1786 duet, No. 20b, should begin with the same four-note motive in the same dotted rhythm, the latter with halved note values.

4   On details of certain recitatives see Rushton, ' . . . hier wird es besser seyn, ein blosses Recitativ zu machen . . .' and 'Tonality in Act III of *Idomeneo*'.

5   The progression could be rationalised by taking the second chord as the enharmonic notation of a 'German sixth' (A♭–C–E♭–F♯ for G♭), which would normally resolve back to G. Such 'explanation' happily does not deprive the progression of its strength.

6   Another forty bars, including some magnificent recitative, originally preceded No. 28, but are cut in the autograph; the words are not in the libretto. *NMA* makes this cut; *MW* reproduces the original, uncut version in which the dominant seventh on B♭ (bar 114) was duly resolved onto E♭. Making the cut simply replaces this with the C minor of No. 28. Heartz (*NMA* Vorwort, p. xxiv; facsimile, p. xxxvii) rightly calls this 'un-Mozartian' and proposes instead a diminished seventh on B♮ in bar 114 and a modification to the voice part (*NMA* p. 471).

7 Some references to this arpeggio not otherwise mentioned are: R. 4 (bar 33); No. 24 (the Priest implores clemency, declaring 'The vow is inhuman'); and less clearly, No. 2 (bar 73), marking the return of the first quatrain.

8 The principal study of rhythm as a dramatic sign is W. J. Allanbrook, *Rhythmic Gesture in Mozart: Le nozze di Figaro and Don Giovanni* (Chicago, 1983).

9 Heartz, 'Raaff's Last Aria'. Arbace's aria (No. 22) is in triple time, as is the middle section of No. 27, 'No, la morte'; but if these and 'Torna la pace' were indeed omitted along with the duet No. 20a there remained (both in 1781 and 1786) no triple time between No. 19 and the divertissement. Both triple and compound triple time have a far stronger representation in Mozart's comedies.

10 R. 6, bar 34 in *MW*: bar 12 in *NMA* appendix (the passage is thought to have been omitted even in 1781). This motive Heartz, noting its fusion during No. 23 with motive C, calls the '*duol* motif'; this refers to No. 10a, bar 50, where a variant of it is sung to that word (*Mozart's Operas*, p. 50). No. 10a was omitted, of course, in 1786, somewhat weakening the configuration.

11 See, for example, in the same key, the slow movement of the G minor Symphony, and Tamino's 'Dies Bildnis ist bezaubernd schön'. The idea is not confined to Mozart; it occurs, still in E♭, in the slow movement of Haydn's String Quartet in C minor, Op. 17 no. 4 (1771).

12 The ambiguity of this remarkable invention is fortified by a grammatical risk: the structural pitch at every half-bar lies a (dissonant) perfect fourth above the bass.

13 See Rushton, '. . . hier wird es besser seyn, ein blosses Recitativ zu machen . . .'.

10 Tonality and motive

1 *Mozart-Jahrbuch 1973–4*, p. 82.

2 See Somfai and Heartz in *Mozart-Jahrbuch 1973–4*, and Heartz, 'Tonality and Motif in *Idomeneo*'.

3 Liebner in *Mozart-Jahrbuch 1973–4*, p. 91. Liebner includes Elettra's first aria which, however important in the scheme of the whole, is hardly a turning-point.

4 On this question, within R. 7, and on tonal links within *Idomeneo* in general, see Rushton, 'Tonality in Act III of *Idomeneo*'.

5 Heartz, 'Tonality and Motif', p. 383; Somfai, *Mozart-Jahrbuch 1973–4*, see the plan on p. 90; Kunze, *Mozarts Opern*, p. 124.

6 Numbers referring to breezes in *Zaide* and *Così fan tutte* are also in E major. However, in the latter, so is a *buffo* trio and Fiordiligi's introspective 'Per pietà'.

7 I have discussed this motive more fully, listing over thirty occurrences and comparing the comments of other critics, in '"La vittima è Idamante": Did Mozart have a Motive?'

8 Cairns, *Responses*, p. 63.

9 Floros, 'Das "Programm" in Mozarts Meisterouvertüren', p. 152.

10   *Ibidem.*
11   See Rushton, '"La vittima è Idamante": Did Mozart have a Motive?'.
     Elettra is, of course, obsessed with Idamante; a consciously leitmotivic
     composer would have made these allusions obvious, whereas they are
     neither exact nor (except in No. 13), very prominent. As the chorus
     flees from the monster, Idamante is hardly in the forefront of any-
     one's mind. A more persuasive reason for the undeniable presence of
     a relation of motive C is the function of No. 18 as a dark parody of
     the overture.
12   Where motive A is concerned, it may be pertinent that descending
     arpeggios covering a sixth, without glissandi, open the Act I and Act
     III choruses 'Nettun s' onori' and 'Scenda Amor', which do honour
     to gods, and the great Chaconne. This is also the head-motive of 'Fuor
     del mar', but for such a commonplace figure it would be difficult to
     argue convincingly for a very definite signification.
13   See chapters 11 and 12 and Rushton, 'A Reconciliation Motive in
     Idomeneo?'
14   Liebner, *Mozart on the Stage*, p. 69.

11   Elettra's first aria and the storm scene

1   William Mann, *The Operas of Mozart*, p. 266.
2   Varesco's failings as a librettist caused Mozart much trouble, espe-
    cially in Act III (see p. 39, above), and have often been discussed since
    (see, for example, Edward J. Dent, *Mozart's Operas* (1947), 33–44). In
    the case of the aria and storm scene, Mozart has turned dramatic
    awkwardness to musico-dramatic advantage: what appears in the
    libretto as an inconsistency becomes, in Mozart's treatment, pure
    music drama.
3   The multiple versions of this pronouncement are discussed in chapter
    2 p. 41, above.
4   Webster, 'Mozart's Operas and the Myth of Musical Unity'. An
    example of the conventional search for tonal structural coherence in
    Mozart's operas is found in Heartz, 'Tonality and Motif in *Idomeneo*'.
5   See p. 138, above.
6   The term 'counterstructure' originates with Christopher Wintle; see
    'Kontra-Schenker: Largo e mesto from Beethoven's Op. 10, No. 3',
    Music Analysis 4 (1985), 145–82. For a specific discussion of the issues
    of unity and discontinuity in Mozart's operas see Webster, 'To
    Understand Verdi and Wagner We Must Understand Mozart', and
    'Mozart's Operas and the Myth of Musical Unity'.
7   For discussion of the treatment of the binary aria form in *Idomeneo*
    see Hirschberg, 'Formal and Dramatic Aspects of Sonata Form in
    Mozart's *Idomeneo*' and chapters 7–8, above.
8   See Julian Rushton, *W. A. Mozart: Don Giovanni* (Cambridge, 1981),
    101–2.

12   Conclusions

1 Hocquard, *Idomenée*, p. 210. Hocquard also points out (p. 107) that Idomeneo (in the recitative before No. 12) infers that the gods are angry with his son for freeing the Trojans; and that is why he had he misfortune to be the first to meet his father. Neptune, however, was on the side of Troy (hence his anger with Idomeneus); his ultimate favouring of Idamante is thus explicable as a reward for the prince's kindness to the Trojan remnant.

2 Kerman's account of *Idomeneo* is included only in the second edition of *Opera as Drama*, pp. 80–5. His conclusion, that *Idomeneo* is 'consistently brilliant, continually beautiful, only sporadically dramatic . . . a work of genius that overflows its theatrical genre' should be read in the light of Kerman's implicit and general rejection of eighteenth-century dramatic forms.

3 See Heartz, 'Mozart, his Father, and *Idomeneo*'.

4 Hocquard, *Idomenée*, p. 214. The relationship between Mozart and Leopold was relatively easy at the time *Idomeneo* was composed; the attempt to deepen understanding by psycho-biographical interpretation actually works better with *Don Giovanni*, precisely through its oblique operation: the Commendatore is not, in fact, Don Juan's father.

5 On the Christian interpretation, see K. Kramer, 'Antike und christliches Mittelalter in Varescos *Idomeneo*'. On the choice of ending, we have no knowledge; it is merely sentimental to suggest that, since it is an improvement, Mozart must have thought of it himself.

6 H. Abert, *W. A. Mozart* I: 854.

7 See F. W. Sternfeld, 'Expression and Revision in Gluck's *Orfeo* and *Alceste*', in *Essays for Egon Wellesz* (London: Oxford University Press, 1966).

8 Hocquard (*Idomenée*, pp. 71–2) describes Elettra as 'a fury who plays an entirely passive role', and justifies her musical importance as having a 'function analogous to the role of the choruses: to confer on the work its high tragic character'.

9 The effect uncannily anticipates Aeneas' great monologue in Act V of Berlioz's *Les Troyens*. Yet there is little evidence that Berlioz knew *Idomeneo* well.

10 Imitation appears in a quasi-symphonic context in the middle of No. 12 ('Fuor del mar', from bar 84). No. 20b (the revised love duet) and the Quartet employ close imitation between voices, where the effect is of developmental intensification. Only in 'Popoli! a voi l'ultima legge' is the imitation not concerned with intensification of a topic, but is engaged as a topic in its own right.

Select bibliography

Abbate, C. and Parker, R. 'Dismembering Mozart', *Cambridge Opera Journal* 2 (1990), 187–95
Abert, A. A. 'Mozarts Italianità in *Idomeneo* und *Titus*', *Analecta Musicologica* 18 (1978), 204–16
  Die Opern Mozarts (Wolfenbüttel, 1970); Eng. trans. 'The Operas of Mozart' in E. Wellesz and F. W. Sternfeld, *The Age of Enlightenment* (*New Oxford History of Music* VII; Oxford, 1973), 97–172
Abert, H. W. A. *Mozart* (6th edn of Jahn, *Life of Mozart*; Wiesbaden, 1924)
Anderson, E., ed and trans. *Letters of Mozart and his family* (London, 1938; rev. 2nd edn, 1966, by A. H. King and M. Carolan; rev. 3rd edn, 1985, by S. Sadie and F. Smart) (see also Bauer)
Angermüller, R. 'Bemerkungen zum *Idomeneus*-Stoff', *Mozart-Jahrbuch 1973–4* pp. 279–97
  '*Idomeneo* auf der Opern- und Schauspielbühne des 18. und frühen 19. Jahrhunderts', and 'Editionen, Aufführungen und Bearbeitungen des *Idomeneo*', in *Bayerische Staatsbibliothek 1981*, pp. 44–61 and 134–57
  Mozart: Die Opern von der Uraufführung bis heute (Frankfurt-am-Main, 1988) Eng. trans. *Mozart's Operas* (New York, 1988)
L'Avant-scène Opéra 89 (1986) *Idoménée.*
Bauer, W. A. and Deutsch, O. E. *Mozarts Briefe und Aufzeichnungen*, 7 vols. (Kassel, 1962–75)
Bayerische Staatsbibliothek 1981 Wolfgang Amadeus Mozart: 'Idomeneo' 1781–1981. Essays, Forschungsberichte, Katalog mit der Rede zur Eröffnung der Ausstellung von Wolfgang Hildesheimer, essays edited by Rudolph Angermüller and Robert Münster (Munich, 1981) (some articles are listed under their authors)
Böhm, K. 'Aufführungspraxis der Opera Seria am Beispiel des *Idomeneo*', *Wissenschaft und Praxis* (Zurich, 1958), 17
Cairns, D. '*Idomeneo*', in *Responses* (London, 1973), 55–77
Dent, E. J. *Mozart's Operas: A Critical Study* (London, 1913; revised 2nd edn, 1947; reprinted Oxford, 1973)
Deutsch, O. E. *Mozart: A Documentary Biography* (London, 1965)
Dietrich, M. '"Wiener Fassungen" des *Idomeneo*', *Mozart-Jahrbuch 1973–4*, pp. 56–76
Eisen, C. *New Mozart Documents* (London, 1991)
Floros C. 'Das "Programm" in Mozarts Meisterouvertüren', *Studien zur Musikwissenschaft: Beihefte zu Denkmäler der Tonkunst in Österreich*

26 (1964), 140–86; revised version in C. Floros, *Mozart-Studien I: Zu Mozarts Sinfonik, Opern- und Kirchenmusik* (Wiesbaden, 1979)

Gerstenberg, W. 'Betrachtungen über Mozarts *Idomeneo*', in T. Kohlhase and V. Scherlies, eds. *Festschrift Georg von Dadelsen zum 60. Geburtstag* (Stuttgart, 1978), 148–54

'Die Musik im *Idomeneo*', in *Bayerische Staatsbibliothek 1981*, pp. 122–33

Gianturco, C. *Mozart's Early Operas* (London, 1981)

Girdlestone, C. *La Tragédie en musique (1673–1750) considérée comme genre littéraire* (Geneva and Paris, 1972)

Goerges, H. *Das Klangsymbol des Todes im dramatischen Werk Mozarts* (Munich, 1937 reprinted 1965)

Greither, A. *Die Sieben Grossen Opern Mozarts* (Heidelberg, 1956, enlarged 2nd edn, 1970; 3rd edn, 1977)

Grout, D. J. *Mozart in the History of Opera* (Washington, 1972)

Heartz, D. 'The Genesis of Mozart's Idomeneo', *Mozart-Jahrbuch 1967*, pp. 150–64 and *The Musical Quarterly* 55 (1969), 1–19; revised in *Mozart's Operas*, pp. 15–36

'Vorwort', in *Neue Mozart Ausgabe* II:5/xi (Kassel, 1972)

'Idomeneus Rex', *Mozart-Jahrbuch 1973–4*, pp. 7–15

'Raaff's Last Aria: A Mozartean Idyll in the Spirit of Hasse', *The Musical Quarterly* 60 (1974), 517–43

'Tonality and Motif in *Idomeneo*', *The Musical Times* 115 (1974), 382–6: also in *Mozart-Jahrbuch 1973–4*, pp. 93–7 and 140–2

'The Invention of *Idomeneo*', *About the House* (Friends of Covent Garden Ltd), V/4 (Christmas 1977), 36–43; as 'Hat Mozart das Libretto zu *Idomeneo* ausgewählt?' in *Bayerische Staatsbibliothek 1981*, pp. 62–70

'Mozart, his Father and *Idomeneo*', *The Musical Times* 119 (1978), 228–31

'Mozart and his Italian Contemporaries: *La clemenza di Tito*', *Mozart-Jahrbuch 1978–9*, pp. 275–93, reprinted in *Mozart's Operas*, pp. 299–318

'The Great Quartet in Mozart's *Idomeneo*', *Music Forum* 5 (1980), 233–56

'Mozart's Tragic Muse', *Studies in Music* (University of Western Ontario) 7 (1982), 183–96, revised and expanded in *Mozart's Operas*, pp. 37–65

'*Idomeneo* and the Tradition of Sacrifice Drama', *Glyndebourne Festival Programme Book 1985*, pp. 139–45, revised in *Mozart's Operas*, pp. 1–14

'"Attacca subito": Lessons from the Autograph Score of *Idomeneo*, Acts I and II'. *Festschrift Wolfgang Rehm zum 60. Geburtstag*, eds. D. Berke and H. Heckmann (Kassel, 1989), 83–92

Mozart's Operas (Berkeley, University of California Press, 1990)

Hell, H. 'Die *Idomeneo*-Bearbeitung von Ermanno Wolf-Ferrari (1931)', in *Bayerische Staatsbibliothek 1981*, pp. 180–201

Hirschberg, J. 'Formal and Dramatic Aspects of Sonata Form in Mozart's *Idomeneo*', *The Music Review* 38 (1977), 192–210

Hocquard, J. -V. *Idoménée* (Paris, 1980)

Höslinger, C. 'Die ersten Aufführungen des *Idomeneo* in Wien, 1786, 1806', *Mozart-Jahrbuch 1986*, pp. 25–8

Jahn, O. *The Life of Mozart* (London, 1882: Eng. trans. of *W. A. Mozart* (Leipzig, 1856))
Keller, H. 'The Idomeneo Gavotte's Vicissitude', *The Music Review* 14 (1953), 155–7
'*Idomeneo*', *The Music Review* 20 (1959), 296–9
Kerman, J. *Opera as Drama* (2nd edn, New York and London 1989)
Kohler, S. 'Die *Idomeneo*-Bearbeitung von Lothar Wallerstein und Richard Strauss (1931)' in *Bayerische Staatsbibliothek 1981*, 158–79
Kramer, K. 'Giovanni Battista Varesco: Versuch eine Biographie', *Acta Mozartiana* 27 (1979/I), 2–15
'Antike und christliches Mittelalter in Varescos *Idomeneo*'; 'Frauenge-stalten in Varescos *Idomeneo*'; and 'Zur Entstehung von Mozarts *Idomeneo*', *Mitteilungen der Internationalen Stiftung Mozarteum Salzburg* 28 (February 1980), 6; and 28 (August 1980), 16; and 29 (September 1981), 23
'Das Libretto zu Mozarts *Idomeneo*: Quellen und Umgestaltung der Fabel', in *Bayerische Staatsbibliothek 1981*, pp. 7–43
Kunze, S. *Mozarts Opern* (Stuttgart, 1984)
Landon, H.C. Robbins, ed. *The Mozart Compendium* (London, 1990)
Lert, E. *Mozart auf dem Theater* (Berlin and Leipzig, 1921)
Liebner, J. *Mozart on the Stage* (London, 1972)
Mann, W. *The Operas of Mozart* (London, 1977)
Mozart-Jahrbuch 1973–4 ('Themenkreis *Idomeneo*') See under separate authors, and the symposium 'Tonartenplan und Motivstruktur (Leitmotivtechnik?) in Mozarts Musik', subsections (1) ('Der Tonartenplan in den Opern mit besonderer Berücksichtigung des *Idomeneo*', 82–97) and (4) ('Das Problem der Leitmotivtechnik in den Opern', 131–44)
Münster, R. 'Mozarts Münchener Aufenthalt 1780/81 und die Uraufführ-rung des *Idomeneo*', in *Bayerische Staatsbibliothek 1981*, pp. 71–105
'Das Münchener *Idomeneo*-Orchester von 1781', in *Bayerische Staats-bibliothek 1981*, pp. 106–21
'Neues zum Münchener *Idomeneo* 1781', *Acta Mozartiana* 25 (1982), 10–20
Neville, D. '*Idomeneo* and *La clemenza di Tito*. Opera seria and vera opera', *Studies in Music* (University of Western Ontario) 8 (1983), 107–36; 10 (1985), 25–49
Noske, F. 'Zur Semantik der Orchestration in Mozarts Opern', *Mozart-Jahrbuch 1978–9*, pp. 88–94
Paumgartner, B. 'Die beiden Fassungen des *Idomeneo*', *Musica* 9 (1955), 423
Platoff, J. 'Writing about Influences: *Idomeneo*, a Case Study', in E. Narmour and R. Solie, eds. *Explorations in Music, the Arts, and Ideas: Essays in Honor of Leonard B. Meyer* (Stuyvesant, N.Y., 1988), 43–65
Ratner, L. G. *Classic Music: Expression, Form and Style* (New York, 1980)
Rushton, J. '"La vittima è Idamante": Did Mozart have a Motive?' *Cambridge Opera Journal* 3 (1991), 1–21
'Tonality in Act III of *Idomeneo*', *Studies in Music* (University of Western Ontario), forthcoming

'A Reconciliation Motive in *Idomeneo?*', *Proceedings* of the Mozart conference at Hofstra University, February 1991, forthcoming

'"' . . . Hier wird es besser seyn – ein blosses Recitativ zu machen . . . "': observations on recitative-organization in *Idomeneo*', in Sadie, S., ed. *Proceedings of the 1991 London Mozart Conference*, forthcoming

Sadie, S. *The New Grove Mozart* (London, 1982)

Saint Foix, G. de *W. A. Mozart: sa vie musicale, son œuvre* III (Paris, 1936)

Valentin, E. ' . . . Punkte, die die Opera betreffen', *Acta Mozartiana*, 28 (1981), 49–54

Webster, J. 'To Understand Verdi and Wagner We Must Understand Mozart', *19th-century Music* 11 (1987–8), 175–93

'Mozart's Operas and the Myth of Musical Unity', *Cambridge Opera Journal* 2 (1990), 197–218

'The Analysis of Mozart's Arias', in C. Eisen, ed. *Mozart Studies* (Oxford, 1991), 101–200

Wolf, E. 'The Mannheim Court', in Zaslaw, N., ed. *The Classical Era* (London, 1989), 233–9

Index

(*Principal references are set in bold.*)